i

Contents

CHAPTER 1

I Introduction

1.1 Introduction

If you are reading this book, congratulations! You have successfully received an interview from one of the amazing vet schools in the UK. Now it is time for the hard bit … preparing.

Filled with top tips and tricks, this specially designed book for aspiring vets is what you need to pass the interview stage and gain a place at your dream vet school. We will take you through the process step-by-step and tell you everything you need to know, from the different interview formats, types of questions and how to answer them, the selection criteria for every vet school in the UK, key do's and don'ts, and plenty of practice questions for you to use in your preparation.

While there is no easy fast-track to success, this book is here to help you put your best foot forward for that all-important interview.

So, let us begin!

Applying to veterinary medicine can be tough! The course is super competitive, there's only one shot at your exams and in your interview with all candidates in these fields scoring high against you. Don't take a chance on your application, let the expectations here at Medic MInd help you achieve success and do your best!

CONTENTS

- Expert advice
- Common pitfalls
- Timing tips
- Numerous example questions with feedback and a runthrough
- Worked MMI stations
- Over 120 sample questions
- How to focus your preparation
- Hot topics

This book has been co-authored by a student who received offers from every interview alongside other vet students who were successful in passing their interview.

1.2 A Beginner's Guide to Veterinary Interviews

The Basics

As there are only 11 vet schools in the UK, applying to veterinary medicine is a very competitive and rigorous process where demand exceeds supply when securing a place on this course. To deal with the increasing competition for places, vet schools have developed new and innovative interview methods, including multiple mini interviews, panel interviews, and situational judgement examinations, to ensure that only the very best candidates are selected from each applicant pool. These interview methods may seem daunting at first, especially if the vet schools you are applying to all use different interview formats. However, while the interview style may differ between vet schools, it is important to remember that they are all ultimately looking for the same qualities. This book will take you through each of these qualities step-by-step, so do not stress!

This book has been put together by a special selection of veterinary graduates and veterinary students, to not only help you to prepare and pass your interview but to also teach you how to enjoy and get the most out of it. No matter your background, what vet school you decide to apply to, or even what type of vet you eventually want to be, this book covers traditional questions and practical stations, as well as necessary background knowledge and tried-and-tested expert advice to help you score highly in the interview process.

The 11 UK vet schools

- Aberystwyth
- Bristol
- Cambridge
- Edinburgh
- Glasgow
- Harper & Keele
- Liverpool
- Nottingham
- RVC
- Surrey
- UClan

Selection Criteria

Every vet school publishes a list of selection criteria for applicants on their website. The selection criteria often echoes interview mark schemes as it represents the qualities that each vet school is assessing applications for. Selection criteria can vary between vet schools, so you should make sure to research each school you are attending interviews at.

The selection criteria for three vet schools is displayed below to demonstrate a handful of key potential differences.

Royal Veterinary College

You will need to demonstrate that you can:

- Take initiative in your research
- Work well as part of a team
- Be organised and prioritise effectively
- Solve challenging problems
- Adapt your communication to a range of situations
- Think creatively about your work experience and how this impacts your role as a vet

University of Liverpool

You will need to demonstrate:

- Critical thinking and decision-making skills
- An understanding of veterinary ethics
- Data manipulation skills
- Veterinary skills and qualities
- Strong motivation to study Veterinary Medicine

Harper-Keele Vet School

You will need to demonstrate:

- Animal handling skills
- An understanding of veterinary ethics
- Teamwork and role playing skills
- Personal skills and qualities - this is what you have to show you can be a vet such as having empathy or good communication skills
- Data interpretation skills

Disclaimer

Please note that the information above is valid and correct as of October 2022 according to the Veterinary Schools Council. This information is subject to change and so, we strongly advise applicants to consult the universities directly.

vetschoolcouncil.ac.uk

What are the interviewers looking for?

Before your interview, the only information vet schools have about you is from your personal statement. Given your personal statement can only be 4,000 characters (roughly one side of A4) there is a lot about you that they still do not know!

The purpose of the interview is for your chosen university to find out more about you as a student, your motivations to study the course, and what you have to offer. The interview questions you come across will vary from university to university, as well as year on year. Some of the skills and knowledge assessed includes but is not limited to...

- Your attitude towards animal welfare
- Your knowledge of current veterinary affairs
- Your decision-making skills
- Your ability to work under pressure

Duties of a Vet

Clients and their patients must be able to trust vets with their lives and health. To justify that trust, you must show respect for animal life as well as respecting the human-animal bond. You must also meet the standards expected of you in four domains, described below.

Knowledge, skills and performance

- Make the care of your patient your primary concern.
- Keep your professional knowledge and skills up to date.
- Recognise and work within the limits of your competence.

Safety and quality

- Take prompt action if you think that patient safety, dignity or comfort is being compromised.
- Protect and promote the health of patients and the public. The one health approach (which concerns the health of animals and humans in their shared environment) is extremely important in veterinary medicine.

Communication, partnership and teamwork

- Treat patients and their owners as individuals and always be respectful of their human-animal bond.
- Treat clients politely and considerately.
- Respect the patient's and owner's right to confidentiality.
- Work in partnership with clients.
- Give clients the information they want or need in a way they can understand.
- Respect the client's right to reach decisions with you about their pet's treatment and care.
- Work with colleagues in the ways that best serve the patient's interests.

Maintaining trust

- Be honest and open and act with integrity.
- Never discriminate unfairly against patients, clients or colleagues.
- Never abuse your client's trust in you or the public's trust in the profession.

During any vet school interview the above listed qualities will be tested in multiple scenarios. These domains represent the many soft skills expected of a trainee vet, and vet school applicants are expected to reflect on their own experiences within the boundaries of these skills. We will explore how to achieve this in more detail in the 'Personal Qualities & Skills' section of this book.

1.3 Types of Interview

Interview structure

The style of interview varies considerable between vet schools. Many vet schools now use multiple mini interviews (MMIs), which involve a series of individually assessed stations testing a variety of skills. However, some universities still use traditional panel interviews which take on a more conversational format. You should identify the interview structure each vet school you have applied to uses, so that you can tailor your preparation accordingly. Please bear in mind that universities have the right to change interview styles and structures between years, so information regarding previous application cycles may not be applicable to you. Ensure you read all communication directly from the vet school about your interview very carefully to ensure you know what to expect on the day.

Multiple Mini Interviews (MMIs)

Also colloquially known as MMIs, multiple mixed interviews offer a 'speed-dating' approach with your interviewer. Typically, there are around 5 MMI stations in an MMI interview. These will be held one after the other with each station assessing different skills and displaying different formats. For example, one MMI station might test your anatomy knowledge by presenting you with two diagrams, cadavers or real-life skeletons! where you may need to compare and explain the skeletal anatomy of a horse vs a dog. However, your MMI station after this may test your understanding of ethics by presenting you with an ethical dilemma and asking how you would respond. Along with these skills and knowledge based stations, you will likely also be asked more traditional interview questions such as why you want to study Veterinary Medicine or why you wish to study at that particular university.

Some universities will offer a short section of reading time (usually 1 minute) prior to each station in order to prepare your answer, particularly if the station is based on a sample of a reading material or a diagram that you need to review and answer questions on. For those universities which do not offer this, you should start preparing your answer on pen and paper if available as the interviewer is running you through the question. Preparing your answer this way allows for a concise and well-thought out response. One great advantage of the MMI interview system is how performance and scores in each interview is collected and reviewed. Performed poorly in your team work station? Do not stress and move on!

The best approach to the MMI is to take each station like it is your first - do not get hung up on mistakes previously made as your interviewer for station 5 will never ever know that you did not know how to label the hind limb skeleton in station 3. Keep calm and focus on the next station.

The vet schools currently adopting this MMI system include:
- Edinburgh
- Harper-Keele
- Liverpool
- Surrey
- RVC

Panel interviews

The most traditional form of interview is made up of multiple interviewers asking a series of questions and the entire interview can range from 20-40 minutes long. The number of people on the panel ranges from 2-3 and can be a good mix of personnel. This may include older vet students on the course, professors at the university, and clinical vets themselves. Unlike MMIs, panel interviews feel less time pressured, as they will feel very conversational and you can refer back to comments made in previous questions to help you answer the next one. This is why some students prefer a panel interview, as you can build on your answers with each question that is asked and potentially feel more focused and therefore more calm.

Virtual interviews

During the Covid-19 pandemic, many universities transitioned to virtual interviews.
In the coming years, we expect vet schools to revert back to in-person interviews. However, some universities may continue to make use of virtual interviews for international applicants for example. Currently most vet schools will interview online following the unexpected 2021-22 pattern so students should be prepared for an online interview. One simple tip to help stay engaged in a virtual interview is to stick a small post-it note with a smiley face on directly next to your webcam, reminding you to stay professionally engaged by making eye contact; the smiley face can also be a useful reminder to smile! This ensures the interviewer knows you are listening and enjoying the process.

Mixed interviews

Due to there being no requirement to sit the UCAT or BMAT for the vet school application, mixed interviews are common when reviewing vet school applications. After submitting your personal statement, some UK vet schools (currently Surrey and Nottingham) will send out a Situational Judgement Test (SJT). As well as being done pre-interview, situational judgement assessments may be done at the beginning of a panel interview. It is important to know that this is just another way vet schools assess students to be able to pick the best out of the many. A situational judgement assessment simply assesses how you will respond and subsequently act as a vet.

Essentially, the SJT puts you in different scenarios and assesses you on how you act and deal with the situation at hand. Although not all the scenarios will be related to Veterinary Medicine, you should keep in mind that your answer should follow the basic ethics and values of a vet.

For example, a non-related vet SJT question could be 'You are sitting an exam and notice a friend sitting beside you is looking over at your answers and copying you… what do you do?'

With this type of scenario-based question, you may be presented with a list of possible responses you could take. For example:

- I would do nothing as it is none of my business if someone cheats
- I would immediately tell the teacher that the student is copying me
- I would wait till the end of the exam and tell the head teacher that they were copying me
- I would wait until after the exam to talk to the student, to inform them that copying is cheating and they should tell the teacher about the situation.

You are then asked to rank these in order of most to least appropriate, and your order will be assessed on the basis of what is actually deemed appropriate.

1.4 Preparing for your Interview

Research the university

Vet schools want to know why you want to study at their institution specifically, to ensure you have thought carefully about your decision to apply, genuinely believe their vet school is right for you, and will therefore hopefully be a hardworking student and an asset to the cohort. You may also be asked why you chose this Vet school over another. As there are limited Vet schools, this is a likely question. You need to ensure you have enough knowledge about the vet school's curriculum, and any unique features of their course, in order to answer well. Different Vet schools teach in different styles, so you should be prepared to explain why their style is best suited for you.

Additionally, it is fundamental to consider the location of the university, and to explain why you are looking forward to spending 5 years there. If you have a particular hobby, sport, or passion, ensure you show that you can offer this to your chosen university. Interviewers love to see this as it shows you have a great work-life balance, which is important to have as a vet to ensure you avoid burn-out and can cope with the high pressure course.

Keep up to date

The veterinary world is constantly changing each and every day, with challenges and new developments that will impact your career. Therefore, you need to show you not only have a great understanding of these issues but also are still interested and keen to learn more about the veterinary world. By reading veterinary blogs (such as the Vet Times) and research papers (such as ScienceDirect) you are able to submerge yourself into the wonderful world of veterinary medicine and will be able to uphold a conversation with any senior vet.

1.5 How to Use This Book

This book was written by a selection of vets and veterinary students who have successfully interviewed at, or sat on interview panels of, some of the top vet schools in the UK. With our collective experiences, we have created an interview resource that students can use to practice questions and feel more confident stepping into the interview room.

Throughout the book you will find three types of text boxes with extra material. An explanation of these text boxes can be found below.

Expert's Advice

Here, our vet interview advisors explain key pieces of advice that candidates may use to better their performance in their interviews. Often, the content of these boxes is what will help distinguish between the strong applicants and the weak ones.

Timing Tip

As the name suggests, these learning points refer to strategies that can be used to circumvent the strict time pressures of the MMI. These have been strategically devised to aid applicants in overcoming one of the greatest challenges in the UCAT - time - without sparing a single mark.

Common Pitfall

Our final focal point discusses the most common mistakes that applicants make at interviews. Through years of successfully tutoring students like yourself, our experts have constructed a roster of much-needed fixes to commonly encountered problems. We strongly suggest reflecting on these points to avoid making the same, or similar, mistakes yourself.

The following chapters form the core content of the book, with information, answer structure advice, and practice questions. As you progress through the book think about how you would answer each question - remember any worked answers given in this text are **not** the only good response. We intended the model answers to be used as a guide to help structure your own response based on your unique life experiences. Every answer you give should be personal to you and demonstrate your own personal motivations. It would be a good idea to start an interview notebook and create bullet point lists of how you would approach each answer.

Ultimately the aim of this handbook is to provide vet school applicants with a guide to interviews containing the information that once helped us all pursue our dreams. We hope that you find it helpful and look forward to welcoming you as colleagues one day.

Good luck!

CHAPTER 2

II Motivation for Veterinary Medicine

2.1 Introduction

The one question that is almost guaranteed to feature in any vet school interview is one that explores a candidate's motivations to pursue a career in veterinary medicine. It may seem clichéd, but there is good reason for interviewers to explore your intentions. Becoming a vet is a huge undertaking and vet schools have a responsibility to only select students with a genuine interest and understanding of the career. Exploring your motivations, and understanding the reasons you are here, is a key aspect of the interview, so it is important to have something prepared.

Your answers to this section of questions will be personal to you. There are no right or wrong answers, and it is important to fully reflect on your own motivations before beginning to draft an answer. Whilst we cannot draft answers on behalf of candidates, we will explore tips and techniques to help structure a well-received answer as well as ways in which to explore personal motivations in a clear and structured manner.

Commonly asked questions

When exploring your motivations for a vet career directly, interviewers will often ask several follow-up questions. Assessors are looking for candidates to demonstrate that they have a realistic understanding of the career, and that they have made an **informed decision** by considering both the positive and negative aspects of the profession.

Example follow-up questions may include the following.

- If you are interested in science, why not become a laboratory scientist or researcher?
- Why would you want to be a veterinary surgeon over a veterinary nurse or other member of the healthcare team?
- What do you wish to achieve in your career, outside of clinical practice?
- Are there any aspects of the vet career that you are not looking forward to? How would you manage this?
- What steps have you taken to explore or further your interest in veterinary medicine?

Common Pitfall

It is important to read the underlying intention behind the question being asked. For questions about your motivations for pursuing veterinary medicine, often an interviewer is looking to see if a candidate understands what they are getting into, speaks of both the positives and negatives, and gives a realistic expectation of veterinary medicine as a career. Try to understand why a question is being asked and tailor your answer to this.

The key point to remember when answering questions about motivation for veterinary medicine is that it is not clear cut. While it is important to have a well prepared answer, you should be prepared for interviewers to scrutinise your response with follow-up questions. Whilst you are preparing your answer, try to anticipate areas that interviewers may ask you to expand on in more depth and prepare for this.

2.2 Why Veterinary Medicine?

It is very likely that this question will be asked at some point during your interview. It is important to consider your genuine motivations that have driven your decision to apply to vet school. Your answer should be personal to you.

Simultaneously, vet schools are looking for candidates to demonstrate a passion or genuine interest in veterinary medicine, as well as a realistic understanding of the career. Therefore, your answer should be a balance of these two ideas, with specific examples from your work experience to evidence your argument and demonstrate insights you have gained. The interviewers want to see that you have thought about and carefully considered the career prior to applying.

Building an answer

While there is no set list of "correct" arguments to mention, the following points may help formulate a starting point to your answer.

Scientific or academic aptitude

Studying veterinary medicine is based on a fundamental understanding of anatomy and biomedical sciences. Particularly in the early years of vet school, much of your learning will be centred around developing an appreciation for the anatomy and physiology underpinning clinical practice. Having a strong interest in science is expected of vet school applicants, and so, it is not a unique selling point in telling your story to your interviewers. Rather, reflect on the source of this interest. Consider projects, experiments and courses in school - or elsewhere - that sparked a passion for science and delve into this, instead of simply stating an interest in science. If you did an EPQ in something veterinary/ animal science-related, this would be a great time to integrate this!

Expert's Advice

Reflection is a key component of a good vet school interview answer. When it comes to motivation for veterinary medicine, consider the ways in which early interests shaped your professional pursuits and may continue to impact your career moving forward. For example, simply stating that caring for your own pet sparked an interest in healthcare will not garner as much interest as exploring the ways in which an understanding of the rise and implication of BOAS (Brachycephalic Obstructive Airway Syndrome) has shaped potential interests moving forward in your career.

Empathy

Being a vet, like most healthcare professions, is ultimately a caring role. It is this aspect of healthcare that separates it from other scientific professions. What is it about this that appeals to you? Perhaps you enjoy the rewarding nature of helping those who cannot help themselves or you have had previous caring responsibilities, which would be good to explore here. Once again, focus on exploring these motivations as opposed to simply stating them; do so with structured examples, anecdotes and more!

Working in a diverse team

- The modern vet rarely works in isolation. Vets not only have to deal with animals (patients) but also need to deal with their human owners (clients) so they need to have a good understanding of how to approach the veterinary-client-patient relationship. Good patient care stems from a group effort involving vets, clients, and other members of the healthcare multidisciplinary team, incorporating many individuals with unique experiences and skills. Even among vets, you will be expected to work with colleagues across different specialties and levels of seniority. Are there any examples where you have enjoyed or thrived working in a team setting? Delve into the qualities that make you both a good leader and a good team player, as these are both vital to a career in veterinary medicine.

Challenging career

The life of a vet is far from easy. A career in veterinary medicine will pose emotional challenges such as dealing with death on a regular basis and having to diagnose rare diseases which can often not be cured. Additionally, veterinary medicine is intellectually, financially, and socially challenging. If, for example, you are a practice owner you need to have the skills not only to be a vet but also how to manage finances and run a successful business. If this challenge appeals to you, make sure you convey this to your interviewers using examples!

Expert's Advice

Focus on communicating a healthy attitude towards challenges and personal growth in your interview. It can be tricky to tow the line between appearing arrogant and coming across as under-confident or easily stressed by a challenge. Reflect on your own experiences to help convey a willingness to be challenged and to learn from your own mistakes.

Varied career

Diagnosing and treating patients is only one of the many possible roles of a vet. There are also opportunities to get involved in teaching, research and management. You might also be looking forward to learning about a wide variety of specialties at vet school, where you will have the chance to try everything from small animal surgery to wildlife conservation medicine. If you have spent time shadowing a vet surgeon, think about the variety of patients and cases seen in a single morning. Is this something you could reflect on and incorporate into your answer?

Timing Tip

Remember that, particularly in MMI stations, you are under time pressure. There are often follow-up questions that need to be answered within the time limit as well. Aim to include 2-3 well explained and detailed points, rather than simply listing multiple arguments without any depth. Answers that prioritise quality over quantity will ensure that there is still time for the interviewer to ask all of their questions.

Sample responses

Example 1

"I want to do veterinary medicine because it is a very prestigious job and will allow me to challenge myself academically as I constantly strive to be the very best in what I do. Additionally, the opportunity to earn good money means I will always be financially secure."

Feedback

This is a poor answer. The student fails to mention anything specific to veterinary medicine and demonstrates no insight into the realities of a career as a vet. The overall impression given here is a candidate motivated by title, prestige and money. Furthermore, there is little to no self-reflection on one's own abilities and skills nor a clear description of their initial inspiration and motivations. Consequently, an interviewer will not be able to glean an accurate portrayal of the candidate's intentions.

Common Pitfall

Interviewers will not be impressed by the mention of money or prestige in any answer to do with motivation for the career. There are many prestigious and well paid jobs aside from veterinary medicine, so this answer suggests that a candidate is not motivated for the right reasons. Furthermore, it may unconsciously remove from the empathetic and altruistic nature of the career by focusing solely on financial incentives. Therefore, this must be avoided at all costs.

Example 2

"I love the academic field of veterinary medicine, and it has been my dream to be a vet since I was very young. My family dog had a life-saving operation when I was 16. This gave me an insight into the intricacies of pet hospital care, and the pressure-driven yet intellectually engaging environment of veterinary medicine."

Feedback

This answer is an average response. The student links lived experience to what they have gained by reflecting on their dog's illness and the ways in which this has influenced their career decisions. Whilst this personal touch is good, it risks coming across as idealistic given the use of words such as "dream" and "love". As a general rule of thumb, avoid mentioning childhood aspirations unless it can be backed up with more recent experiences to demonstrate you have an understanding of both the pros and cons of the career. Veterinary medicine is a complex career and so, childhood dreams and aspirations are rarely an adequate reflection of the profession as it is nearly impossible to know what veterinary practice entails at that age. If mentioning early experiences, ensure that this is described as an initial inspiration that encourages further exploration through work experience and personal research.

Example 3

"Over the past few years, my interest in biology has developed into a passion for veterinary medicine as I gained a greater understanding of the role of a vet in the community. My work experience at my local veterinary practice highlighted the importance of first opinion vets as the first contact for owners of the patients in the community. Viewing the variety of cases the vet had to deal with, and seeing how they logically identified symptoms and asked questions to the owner in order to reach a diagnosis, showed me how veterinary medicine was an intellectually challenging profession that I would relish."

Feedback

This is a good answer. It links together two different, but equally important, sides of being a vet - scientific theory and clinical practice. Including insights gained from work experience provides evidence for the interviewer and shows that the student has been proactive. To further ameliorate this answer, the candidate can further explore the skills they have gleaned from this and other experiences that mimic those required for a successful career in veterinary medicine.

Using evidence in your answer

Answering questions surrounding your motivation for studying veterinary medicine requires you to address two key concepts.

- **Passion for veterinary medicine:** You should show that you are genuinely excited to study veterinary medicine and become a vet.
- **Informed decision:** You need to demonstrate that your passion to be a vet is informed through work experience, individual research, and spending time reflecting on the daily duties of a vet to assess whether you are suitable for the career.

Importantly, your answers should show a balance of these two ideas. A person with a very strong passion for veterinary medicine but with little experience to justify this passion, or vice versa, is unlikely to be successful.

A good way to demonstrate both of these aspects is to use examples from your work experience to back up any points that you make. This shows the interviewer that you have reflected on your experiences and used this to guide your decision - a key skill for future vets! Try to think of a number of examples that you could have on hand to reinforce your answers.

Expert's   Advice
Once you have a good idea of how you would answer a question about your motivation for veterinary medicine, rehearse your answer with others to ensure you can explain yourself easily but do not sound over-rehearsed or robotic. Additionally, you can record yourself going over your response to watch back and critique your own communication skills. Hearing your answer played back can also aid you in picking it apart in a way that will mimic the interviewers.

Practice MMI station

Station brief

What inspired you to want to become a vet?

Tell the interviewer about an animal patient you cared for during work experience or volunteering who inspired you to find out and question their client (owner) about what was wrong with them.

Good answer A good answer may include:

- An interest in science, demonstrating a true passion for learning about anatomy
- A desire to help people, with reference to charity work or other examples illustrating a candidate's altruistic nature
- The social aspect of veterinary medicine, with specific reference to the roles of the human-animal bond and how you interact with the patient and patient's owner
- A reflection on work experience, showing insights gained during placements and how this has informed a decision to apply to vet school
- Personal experience, such as a family pet being unwell with reflections that support previous points

Poor answer

A poor answer may include:

- Unrealistic or idealistic motivations, for example "at age 7 I got a hamster and this inspired me to become a vet"
- Superficial reasons that are unspecific to veterinary medicine, such as talking about a "desire to help animals" without further reference to other aspects of veterinary medicine or linking to charity/volunteering work

2.3 Realities of Becoming a Vet

Ultimately, your end goal in the career should be to become the best vet you can. This is exactly what the interviewer for your vet school will be looking for: the best vet out of all their applicants. As a vet, you need to show that you have a great degree of emotional intelligence. This means you need to not only understand the pros of your life as a vet but also the cons. It is common for the interviewer to ask about both sides to show you understand this. Below are some common advantages and disadvantages which have been highlighted by those in the veterinary profession.

Advantages of a career in Veterinary Medicine

- **Immense job satisfaction and gratification**

  Being a vet gives you the ability to go to work and help patients at a personal level, truly making a difference to animals and their owners lives.

- **Academically challenging career with life long learning**

  Throughout your career, you will constantly be using your academic skills to improve your knowledge and apply this to cases in front of you.

- **Able to combine science with altruism**

  Veterinary medicine not only allows you to understand and apply science at a high level but relies on drawing upon your social and communication skills on a daily basis.

- **Well respected and stable career**

  Generally, veterinary medicine is respected within society and offers a career that is sought-after, always needed and hard to replace. This lends lifelong stability.

- **Opportunities for self-development**

  Treating patients is not the only aspect of a medical career. There are numerous opportunities for a vet to develop their skills, be it through research, teaching or something completely novel!

Disadvantages of a career in Veterinary Medicine

- **Stressful lifestyle with long hours, night shifts and lengthy training pathways**

  This can lead to tension among family and friends who may not understand the nature of the work. It can also cause mental and physical burnout.

- **High pressure environment**

  This is a field where every decision counts, and mistakes may have irreversible consequences.

- **Rude or disrespectful owners**

  Unfortunately, this is inevitable as humans are unpredictable by nature. Furthermore, liaising with people who are upset or stressed will often lead to unfriendly interactions. Vets are constantly under public scrutiny and in some cases, this can lead to complaints, even in situations not under your control.

- **Emotional impact on yourself**

  Not every patient in your care will get better despite your very best efforts. While this is an acknowledged fact of medicine, it can be hard to deal with.

Expert's Advice

When mentioning the negative aspects of veterinary medicine an excellent candidate would also consider how they would personally cope with such challenges. By doing so, a candidate shows initiative and insight into their own capabilities. For example, when mentioning the high stress faced by vets you could discuss how you plan to relax and handle pressure while at medical school. Suicide in the veterinary world is one of the highest amongst professions and is a hot-topic and you may be asked how will you deal with this high statistic. By starting to talk about disadvantages of the career you can then go on to talk about how you will use your hobbies/interests to combat this and maintain a healthy well-being during your time as a vet.

Approaching questions about positives and negatives

The key to answering questions about the positive and negative aspects of veterinary medicine is to remain **balanced**. You should not come across as overly positive as this gives a naive and unrealistic impression, suggesting that you have not considered the realities of life as a vet. Likewise, an answer that is overwhelmingly negative paints you in a cynical light and can lead interviewers to question why you have applied.

Good candidates will draw on their observations and work experience to answer these questions. For example, if you have shadowed a vet surgeon, mentioning specific positive and negative elements of the placement, such as challenging conversations with owners, demonstrates an ability to reflect and learn from past experiences. This conveys a level of engagement and self-reflection suggesting that you have partaken in the work experience to actively learn from it rather than to ameliorate your application.

When exploring the disadvantages of a career in veterinary medicine, we strongly encourage candidates to discuss the ways in which to combat these challenges whilst conveying a level of personal resilience to showcase an ability to constructively deal with them.

Timing Tip

A useful structure when approaching questions about the realities of veterinary medicine is to give a positive, followed by a negative, followed by another positive and so on. This ensures a balanced response is put forward even if time runs out.

Practice MMI station

Station brief

You are a final year vet student on placement in an equine referral hospital. Your colleague, Deji, is feeling stressed out with his work. He has lost motivation for veterinary medicine and is tired of the negative aspects of the job. Speak to him about his concerns, address the points he makes and emphasise the positive aspects of his job as a vet.

Notes for actor (Deji)

You are frustrated as clients have been shouting at you due to long waiting times all day and this is not your fault. You are not enjoying the equine hospital rotation work, as you prefer doing surgeries rather than diagnostics and physiotherapy. You are finding the hours long and stressful, and you haven not been able to spend any meaningful time with your partner for two weeks.

Good answer

A good answer will:

- Take a balanced approach whilst still being realistic about the advantages and disadvantages mentioned. The role of a vet is never glamorised but the tone is not overly negative either.
- Empathise with Deji. His concerns are valid and should not be dismissed. Good candidates will show him concern and offer support where appropriate.
- Mention non-clinical roles. As Deji is struggling with his clinical workload it is reasonable to remind him of other opportunities available to him as a vet, such as getting involved in teaching or research.

Poor answer

A poor answer will:

- Be unrealistic in the portrayal of veterinary medicine, either too positive or overly negative.
- Give generic advice, unspecific to the situation. In a roleplay scenario you need to respond to what the actor is saying. Mentioning pros and cons not relevant to the specific scenario demonstrates poor listening skills.
- Demonstrate poor communication. While this interview station is assessing your understanding of veterinary medicine pros and cons, you will also be assessed on your communication skills. Answers that do not empathise with Deji's concerns will not score highly no matter the validity of the points made.

2.4 Roles of a Vet

Being a vet in the 21st century is more than just diagnosing illnesses, prescribing treatments and occasional surgeries. A veterinary career is multi-faceted with multiple opportunities available to vets outside of the clinical environment. Additionally, veterinary training enables you to pursue several different paths, allowing vets to tailor their career to their own personal interests alongside clinical work in the specialty of their choice.

Showing an understanding of the variety of roles available in veterinary medicine demonstrates you have fully researched and considered life as a vet and that you have made an informed decision about your own career. This in turn supports your motivation for veterinary medicine as you can reflect on your experiences to show suitability and excitement for multiple aspects of a medicine. While reading the roles of a vet below, consider which non-clinical roles you may be suited to and if you have any experiences - such as work experience or extracurricular activities - that demonstrate this.

Expert's Advice

Reflecting on potential career interests and how these can be pursued whilst at vet schools gives an interviewer an idea of what you can bring to that particular institution. You may even want to research which areas or career types of veterinary medicine each university is particularly known for and relate this to your own personal interests. This demonstrates commitment and consideration of long-term career goals.

General clinical practice

General clinical practice refers to the act of treating and caring for patients. This is often seen as the primary role of a vet and involves various activities such as interpreting investigation results, communicating with owners, and deciding on treatment plans. The majority of vets will be involved in the clinical management of patients to some degree. However, unlike with human GPs, first opinion vets are also required to do surgeries involving a general anaesthetic. Within general clinical practice, there are a range of roles: veterinary surgeons, veterinary nurses, practice manager (usually a vet surgeon) and receptionists.

Government service

Looking at the public sector, veterinarians are not only employed to look after animal health but can also be involved in protecting public health by undertaking the one health approach. As previously mentioned, one health is an approach that recognizes that the health of people is closely connected to the health of animals and our shared environment. This approach means that some vets work for departments and agencies such as Defra (Department for Environment, Food and Rural Affairs). Veterinarians working for Defra have a lot of responsibility, such as control of major epidemic zoonoses from farm animals, monitoring consumer protection, and controlling the import and export of animals for meat consumption.

Teaching

All vets have to act as teachers to some degree, be it through supervising younger vets or explaining a complex disease process to clients. There are also many additional opportunities for vets to become involved in medical education and formally teach veterinary students at vet schools across the country. Consider the skills required by those in educational roles, and how these skills may be demonstrated within the context of your own experiences.

Research

Healthcare provision in the UK is evidence-based, meaning that all clinical interventions are based on robust research studies supporting their use. As such, veterinary medicine can only advance if there is a consistent and robust effort towards scientific advancement and research. Many senior clinical vets work alongside academic staff to conduct experiments to further their particular fields. You can begin to get involved in research as early as vet school if this is something that interests you. You can demonstrate an aptitude for research at your vet school interview by discussing additional study in a topic of personal interest such as an EPQ, summer project, or even simply attending a free virtual course in an area of interest. These activities can all be used as strong evidence of a commitment to research.

Charity and volunteering work

There are many veterinary related charities that rely on the support of vets to continue their valuable work. Some of these in the UK include: RSPCA, PDSA and the Blue Cross. As you may have done some volunteering already as part of your work experience for your application, you can draw on these experiences to reflect on how valuable your skills can be in this sector.

Military practice

The armed forces employ veterinary scientists in the Royal Army Veterinary Corps to care for animals (mainly dogs) used in service. There are also opportunities as an equine vet to care for the horses used for ceremonial purposes. Veterinarians recruited into the army will join with the rank of an army captain for a four-year short service commission.

In addition to this there are also many different types of vet a student may choose to be after their studies. This includes but is not limited to: a small-animal vet (the most popular), large animal vet, equine vet or an avian vet.

This list is not exhaustive as the opportunities available to vets are diverse and constantly evolving. If you have an interest in a particular field or interest in being a particular type of vet, conduct some research and consider how this could be incorporated into a medical career.

Sample responses

What do you wish to achieve in your career in veterinary medicine, aside from clinical practice?

Example 1

"I would like to focus my studies and thus my career on small animal surgery and the hopes of one day owning and running my own first opinion practice. While I was on my work experience placement, I got to shadow the practice owner and ask him about the qualities it takes to run a small animal veterinary clinic. Therefore, when I become a small animal surgeon, I look forward to working my way up to opening a private practice and having a more of a management role as well"

Feedback

This is a poor answer. While the student attempts to reflect on their work experience, they do so superficially and only identify opportunities in the management sector of veterinary medicine. This comes across as money motivated and shows a lack of insight into management opportunities. Furthermore, there are no links to the candidate's own skills to evidence their career motivations.

Example 2

"I hope to become involved in academic research alongside my clinical career. During my work experience placement at a small animal practice, I met a owner who was consenting for their pet (the patient) to take part in a clinical trial due to their condition, which highlighted to me the important interaction of biomedical research and patient care. While researching your veterinary school, I was particularly excited by the opportunity to take an intercalated research year during the degree as this would explore my research interests further and gain valuable experience."

Feedback

This is a good answer. The student identifies a suitable area of non-clinical practice and demonstrates an understanding of why research is important. The student also shows initiative by having plans to become involved in research early in their career. Notably, the candidate mentions opportunities to do so at the vet school in question which echoes a sense of commitment to researching potential career pathways and opportunities. This will be well received by interviewers.

2.5 Extracurricular Activities

In this section we will discuss how to incorporate extracurricular activities into answers about your motivation for veterinary medicine. We talk about extracurricular activities and hobbies in more depth further in the book, but if you have undertaken activities that draw attention to your interest in veterinary medicine then it is a good idea to discuss them when this topic arises.

What extracurriculars should you mention?

When talking about your motivation to be a vet, you need to demonstrate a genuine passion for veterinary medicine. If you can show the interviewers that you have actively taken steps to further explore any interest you have, it displays a degree of proactivity, dedication to the subject, and motivation to learn.

Extracurriculars relevant to your motivation for veterinary medicine could include any of the following.

Research placements

Some universities host summer schools allowing students to conduct short research projects in their labs. Alternatively, if you are a graduate applicant you could mention a research project conducted as part of your degree relevant to a particular area of veterinary medicine that you are interested in.

EPQ and other projects

An EPQ is an additional qualification taken alongside A-Levels requiring the submission of an extended essay on a topic of your choice. If you have taken an EPQ in a veterinary topic, make sure to mention it and reflect on what you learnt. You may also have researched a particular topic in depth for another project such as an essay competition or science fair.

Attending talks

There are numerous free in-person and online talks relevant to veterinary medicine and bioveterinary science. Take a look at university outreach programmes as they may conduct sessions aimed at applicants. You can also find many relevant pre-recorded lectures or podcasts online. Some of the best come from The Royal Dick School of Veterinary Studies, all about animal welfare and what qualities it takes to be a vet. Likewise, on Spotify, RVC have a range of podcasts from lecturers at their university. Make sure you can briefly summarise the topic in 30 seconds as interviewers may want to check your comprehension!

Reading veterinary related books/blogs

Every applicant should read at least one veterinary related book or blog before their interview. There are a plethora available across a broad range of specialties and you should be able to find many of the most popular titles in your local or school library. During the interview, make sure to reflect on what you have read and explain how this has influenced your decision to medicine. It is also wise to recap the reading just before your interview by reading online summaries in case the interviewers try to catch you out. You can find scientific articles related to veterinary studies at ScienceDirect for an in-depth academic approach or you can also read up online and in the Vet Times magazines for all the updates in the veterinary world.

Societies at school

Your school may run a society aimed at aspiring veterinarians. If you have attended any sessions, mention that you are a member and describe the types of activities or workshops involved. If your school does nott have a veterinary society, consider setting one up as this demonstrates great leadership skills!

Volunteering

Any volunteering work taken in a healthcare or caring setting is valuable and demonstrates your commitment to veterinary medicine. Volunteering does not have to be in a veterinary clinic as the majority of volunteering placements demonstrate multiple transferable skills and dedication.

Worked examples

Example 1

"As I have a keen interest in veterinary ethics and its application to clinical practice, I decided to set up a Vet Ethics Society at my school. Every week we discuss current affairs in the veterinary healthcare environment and the importance of being aware. One such recent discussion was on tail-docking of companion dogs."

Feedback

This is a good answer. Here, the student has shown a great deal of enthusiasm for studying veterinary medicine. They have stated they had the motivation to start a society and have also named one of the relevant hot topics to veterinary ethics showing they keep well on top of the news of veterinary medicine.

2.6 Practice Questions: Motivation for veterinary medicine

1. Why do you want to become a vet?
2. What sparked your interest in veterinary medicine?
3. What are the pros and cons of veterinary medicine?
4. Have you thought about what type of vet you would like to be? What is it about this that appeals to you?
5. What are your main goals for your career in veterinary medicine?
6. What other professionals are involved in patient care? What do they do?
7. Describe the role of a vet nurse. How is this different from that of a vet?
8. Why do you want to be a vet rather than a vet nurse?
9. Why do you want to be a vet rather than a veterinary technician?
10. If you couldn't be a veterinarian, what job would you do?
11. What would you do if you were rejected from vet school this year?
12. Describe an interesting recent medical development that you have read about.
13. When you think about becoming a vet, what are you most looking forward to?
14. When you think about becoming a vet, what are you least looking forward to?
15. What impact do you hope to make in the field of veterinary medicine?
16. Do you agree with the statement "veterinary medicine is a vocation"?
17. What is a particular aspect of veterinary medicine that interests you?
18. Would you rather be a small animal vet or a large animal vet?
19. Describe a time where a ver inspired you.
20. Tell me about a veterinary-related book that you have read.
21. What do you think interviewers should be looking for whilst interviewing?
22. How would you dissuade someone from studying veterinary?
23. Why do you think people leave the veterinary profession?
24. Which medical specialty are you least interested in? Why?
25. What does a vet do aside from treating patients?
26. How have you acted on your interests in veterinary medicine?
27. How has your work experience influenced your decision to apply to vet school?
28. What was your favourite part of your work experience?
29. Were there any parts of your work experience that you didn't enjoy?
30. Who is the most important member of a multidisciplinary health care team?

CHAPTER 3

III Work Experience

3.1 Introduction

Work experience in the context of vet school admissions can be defined as any type of activity or life experience which has prepared you for a veterinary medicine career in some way. Although vet schools generally appreciate that work experience can be difficult to obtain, particularly since the pandemic, most vet schools require a minimum number of hours and for you to do certain types of work experience.

For example, RVC currently requires applicants to obtain a total of 70 hours (10 full days) of work experience in one or more veterinary practices, as well as 70 hours in one or more non-clinical working environments with live animals.

You will likely be asked about your work experience directly with questions such as *"What was your favourite part of your work experience?"* However, this is not the only time work experience can be incorporated in your answer. It may be useful to consider work experience as **evidence** that you can use to strengthen most answers. For example, a strong answer to the question *"What are the challenges of working as a vet?"* will use observations from their work experience to support any points made. Try and show off all the interesting work experience you have completed whenever it is relevant!

Why do we need work experience?

There are a number of reasons why vet schools ask applicants to carry out work experience placements, including:

- Gaining a **realistic** understanding of veterinary medicine, including the physical demands of the job, organisation of the clinical environment, and emotional demands of the career.
- Developing values and skills essential to becoming a vet, including communication, teamwork and empathy. We will explore this further in the 'Personal Qualities and Skills' section of this book.
- Demonstrating motivation and commitment to a career in veterinary medicine, which is particularly applicable to long-term placements requiring a significant time commitment.

Keeping these three points in mind when talking about work experience at your interviews will ensure you are providing examples relevant to the competencies interviewers are assessing.

Getting started

When you are conducting your work experience it is useful to keep a diary of your observations and review this prior to any interviews. Similarly, some students like to create a mind map of each placement to reflect on what they saw and learnt and how this could be applied to potential interview questions.

You should aim to have a set of well thought-out and reflected points developed from your work experience that you are prepared to mention in multiple interview scenarios.

Timing Tip

You will not have time to mention every interesting aspect of every work experience placement you have carried out. Be selective about what scenarios you discuss and make sure these are those that display the highest quality reflections. It is much easier to do this if you have prepared in advance.

The remainder of this section will discuss questions relating to the three most common work experience settings: small animal clinic, zoo and large animal/farm.

3.2 Small animal work experience

Work experience at a small animal clinic is where most vet applicants start as the basis of the application. Shadowing a small animal veterinary surgeon is a good way to get an idea of the life of a vet given that nearly 70% of graduates chose this path. More importantly, first opinion small animal practices are where most pets will end up when they first become unwell or have been scheduled for appointments.

What can I expect from small animal work experience?

No two work experience placements are the same and you are not expected to see a minimum number of consultations or complete a set list of activities. However, if you mention undertaking a small animal clinical work experience placement you could be asked about specific aspects of GP care as it is expected that you will have observed, or discussed, common activities that GPs perform during their daily work.

Take a look at your work experience diary and try to find examples where you observed the following aspects of small animal veterinary care.

Same day or emergency appointments

These are for patients who need to be seen urgently and are typically booked into a number of empty slots, kept aside and awaiting a triage approach to fitting them into the daily schedule. Sometimes other veterinarians may also book patients at the end of their clinics too - how do you think they manage this in terms of timing?

Pre-booked or routine appointments

These are for patients with non-urgent problems who can wait days to weeks for appointment slots. This could be used for medication reviews, following-up chronic diseases and delivering routine test results. Did you observe any differences in the types of conditions seen at these appointments?

Telephone consultations

Telephone consultations are being utilised increasingly in both primary and secondary care settings. Can you think of any limitations or benefits of this? If you observed a telephone consultation, think about how the vet adapted their communication style compared to a traditional face-to-face appointment. Additionally, think about which member of the veterinary clinic team took this call - can you say anything about the importance of this and how triaging works in a small animal clinic?

Nurse appointments

 Following on from this, sitting in on nurse clinics is a great way to understand the differences between the job roles of vet nurses and vets. Think about any differences you observed - was this what you expected? You may find nurses carry out more traditional 'vet jobs' than you initially expected! How did this influence your motivation to study veterinary medicine?

Reception work

You may have been presented with the opportunity to sit with a vet receptionist. This provides an appreciation of the impact non-clinical staff can have on patient and client care. Can you think of any examples of good care or communication provided by one of the receptionists?

Practice questions

How do small animal practices prioritise patients?

"As a small animal first opinion vet works under time pressure, it is critical that patients who are more seriously unwell are given priority. When I undertook a work experience placement at my local veterinary practice, patients' owners were initially booked for short telephone consultations. The receptionist and sometimes the vet nurse used these telephone calls to assess the severity of symptoms and determine which patients needed to be seen in-person that day. In some cases the vet surgeon was confident enough to diagnose over the phone, which had the benefit of saving the patient time to come into the clinic.

While the telephone triage system can save time, I recall a scenario where a client became upset with the system as they felt that they had not been properly assessed due to their cat who was unwell not being physically examined. This made me consider the patient and client perspective due to the human-animal bond and how a patient being triaged as non-urgent could be interpreted to the client as receiving a lower standard of care. Some vet practices have opted to use alternative triaging systems for this, among other reasons."

Explanation

This question is looking for candidates to have considered the important task of *triage*, which refers to the process of deciding which order patients should be seen in. The student is able to reflect on their work experience to describe the prioritisation process they observed, while also having an appreciation of positive and negative aspects of the system.

How long did each appointment last for? Did you feel this was an appropriate appointment length?

"Each first opinion vet appointment is typically just 10 minutes long as standard. I found that for some patients this was sufficient to explore their symptoms and recommend a management plan. However, for some patients with more complex, or multiple, issues the 10 minute time slot was restrictive to the amount of depth that could be explored.

For example, I can recall a particular patient, a 4-year old cat ,at her appointment regarding constant itching. The vet skilfully fully explored her symptoms and prescribed a treatment within the appointment slot, but just as the consultation was ending the owner wanted to tell the vet her cat had also been suffering from diarrhoea and wanted to discuss this too. This demonstrates how difficult having such tight time limits can be, as time efficiency must be balanced with showing you care and have time for the patient without them feeling rushed."

Explanation

Vet first opinion appointment times are often difficult to stick to, but 10 minutes is standard across the UK. Owners frequently complain about being called later than their appointment time due to previous appointments over-running which can strain the relationship between vet and client before the appointment has even begun. This question is looking for a student to understand the strain of appointment length on vets and to demonstrate some insight into the challenges this poses for veterinarians.

What is the role and importance of the vet receptionist?

"I was lucky enough to spend an afternoon with the reception team while on my work experience placement in a small animal first opinion practice. I observed the receptionists booking appointments, dealing with client requests and liaising with the veterinarians and nurses when needed. Overall, my time with the reception staff demonstrated the importance of organisation within veterinary healthcare systems, as without the work performed by reception staff the whole system would cease to function."

<u>Explanation</u>

By asking this question, an interviewer is making sure candidates have an understanding and appreciation for the critical work other members of the healthcare team, including non-clinical staff, perform to improve patient care.

What are the skills required by a first opinion small animal vet?

"A vet working in a small animal clinic needs to be knowledgeable and up-to-date in the management of conditions spanning every medical speciality. Additionally, many soft-skills are required for good clinical practice including, open mindedness, time efficiency and the ability to multitask.

During my work experience in this field I particularly noticed the need for a vet to possess strong communication skills. Vets will see a wide variety of patients and clients who have a range of communication needs. The owner is involved, as well as the patient who can't even talk! Communication between the vet and the owner is vital and they need to be as clear as possible so the owner understands what is going on with their pet. A vet needs to be in-tune with and be able to adapt to these varying needs of the human-animal bond within a short timeframe. For example, I recall the vet seeing a border collie patient whose owner trains dogs for the cruft competitions and then in the next appointment just 10 minutes later, they had to communicate to a first time owner of a shih tzu puppy."

<u>Explanation</u>

This question is an excellent opportunity to discuss observations you made during your work experience. There are a vast number of skills you could mention, but try to pick a handful to discuss in depth with support from scenarios in your work experience. An excellent answer would reflect on these experiences and provide examples where they also demonstrate the skill in question.

3.3 Surgical Work Experience

During your small-animal first opinion clinic experience it is more than likely you got to see some surgeries. Most of this will be regular routine surgeries such as neutering or dental work however do include handling some traumatic injuries. Surgery is a key part to being a vet of any kind since as a vet you will be expected to be always involved in surgery no matter the animal or issue at hand.

What can I expect from surgical work experience?

Observing operations

Witnessing operations is probably the aspect of surgery that students look forward to the most. Operations can either be performed as an emergency or elective, meaning they have been planned in advance.

Common pitfall

Remember that work experience is not about what you have done, but rather what you learnt and took away from the experience. Interviewers will not be fooled by candidates who simply list complex procedures they have witnessed in a bid to be impressive. Instead, reflect on the experience including simple interactions between colleagues.

Members of the surgical team

Thinking of a routine spay, the surgical team will consist of the main veterinary surgeon and usually one veterinary nurse. Try and talk to both of these staff members if possible to understand what their role is during surgery and how it impacts the patient and how their owner might be feeling.

Practice questions

Can you tell me about a surgery you have seen?

 "During my work experience at my local veterinary clinic, I was lucky enough to witness a female dog being spayed which the vet surgeon later told me the correct term to be an ovariohysterectomy. The vet nurse, who I got to witness prep the surgery by keeping everything hygienic to avoid unwanted bacterial transmission, told me how this type of surgery was becoming less popular than it was 20 years ago. The veterinary surgeon then went on to tell me the importance of neutering as a form of preventive medicine. Female dogs can develop an infection called pyometra which results in the need for emergency surgery as it can cause death if untreated. As I learnt this only occurs in dogs without having an ovariohysterectomy surgery, it highlighted to me how preventive medicine for patients is in my opinion in their best interest to stop sickness before it starts."

Explanation

The key aspect of this question is to recognise the reasoning behind certain surgeries. The student goes on to talk about preventive medicine which is important in deciding whether surgery is appropriate or not in certain   cases.   Overall   this   is   an   excellent   answer.

What skills does a good vet surgeon have?

"Small animal vet surgeons are required to be knowledgeable, work in a team and have good communication skills. In addition, due to the practical nature of their job, a surgeon must have incredible manual dexterity skills. During my work experience, I was amazed by how small some of the anatomical structures operated on were. This reinforced the importance of precision to a surgeon's work.

I was given the opportunity to observe a cyst removal during my work experience. Unfortunately, there were complications as the patient began to bleed. This scenario, while initially startling to me, demonstrated how a vet surgeon's ability to maintain composure in difficult situations is critical. I noticed how the vet demeanour often sets the tone of the room, which was particularly key in this case as the patient was awake."

Explanation

Different types of vets draw on different skill sets and this question is asking candidate's to reflect on their observations of surgeons to discuss the skills particularly relevant to their job. An excellent candidate would suggest ways in which they have, or plan to, develop these same skills.

Have you read an article or interesting news topic relating to surgery?

"I have recently read an article from the vet times regarding a life threatening incident due to something so common and once thought harmless. An owner has been playing with her dog in the park and had thrown her a stick, once at home and the next day the dog's owner had noticed her dog was fatigued and had blood in her vomit. Once at the vets, it was discovered that the stick had nipped a vital blood vessel in the back of the dog's throat. In order to locate such an intricate blood vessel cut, a team of soft tissue specialists used a video endoscope to identify the entry site of the wound in order to stop excessive bleeding. This was similar to a case I got to see during my work experience where the sharp wood of a stick got caught in a dog's soft padding on their paw. However, as it was an external injury, no intricate entering of the cavity was needed to discover the site of the injury.

Explanation

By showing evidence of further reading around topics relevant to work experience, the candidate is showing they are genuinely interested in veterinary medicine and have the drive to learn more. Similarly a vet student may be expected to use their evenings to read up on conditions they have seen on placement that day. If you are asked a question like this, expect to be asked follow-up questions about your opinions. Consequently, never pretend to have read something you have not!

3.4 Practice Questions: Work Experience

1. What did you learn from your work experience?
2. Can you tell me about a memorable situation you observed, and what you learned from it?
3. What important qualities did you notice from vets during your work experience?
4. Why do you think we want our applicants to have work experience?
5. How did your work experience change your view of the vet clinics or veterinary in general?
6. After an operation, what is the role of the vet team in the patient's care?
7. Apart from the operating theatre, did you shadow the vets in another setting such as a clinic?
8. What do you feel about the telephone triage system used in many first opinion practices?
9. What are the challenges of being a first opinion vet?
10. Do you think vets should have telephone consultations as an option for clients?
11. Do you feel that the public's perception of a vet is misrepresentative?
12. What did you notice about the skills vets needed when they were carrying out a patient history?
13. What did you notice about the vets you were shadowing in their approach to clients?
14. What challenges did you observe the vet face whilst on work experience? How did they overcome them?
15. What is something you observed a vet do during work experience that you would have done differently?
16. What was the most enjoyable part of your work experience?
17. Describe a time that you observed a vet delivering good communication skills.
18. What is something you saw a vet do that you feel could be improved?
19. Who is the most important member of a veterinary healthcare team?
20. Is there anything about how small animal vet clinics are run that you would change?
21. What did you find most surprising whilst doing your work experience?
22. What does the term "holistic care" mean to you?
23. What did the vet do during your work experience that impressed you the most?
24. What did you hope to gain from your work experience?
25. Who inspired you the most during your work experience?
26. Was your work experience what you expected?

CHAPTER 4

IV Personal Qualities & Skills

4.1 Introduction

Questions concerning a candidate's personal qualities and skills are very common in veterinary school interviews. As we discussed in the selection criteria section of this book, veterinary schools are looking for certain qualities and skills you have to show that you will be a good vet. Therefore, interviewers are not only expecting students to identify the skills required of a veterinarian. Candidates are also expected to demonstrate how they have begun developing these skills themselves.

It is important to prepare in advance and reflect on your own personality traits in the context of veterinary medicine. This type of question can take on many different forms so it is useful to use a framework to have a set answer structure to rely on regardless of the type of question asked.

Medic Mind's framework for discussing skills

Students often struggle to construct answers discussing their skills that are effective and succinct. We have evolved a 5-step method of approaching questions that discuss skills and qualities. Our method encourages you to prepare discussion points of several skills, but importantly can be applied to multiple questions and does not appear formulaic and run the risk of sounding ingenuine or robotic.

Step 1: Pick 3 extracurricular activities

Consider all the extracurricular activities you have taken part in over the past few years. Examples could be volunteering, part-time work, hobbies, school societies and clubs among many others. The first step is to select three of these activities that could link to veterinary medicine and showcase your achievements in the best possible light. Try to choose areas that are sufficiently different and do not overlap by demonstrating similar skills.

Example

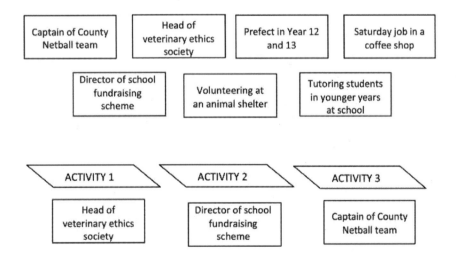

Step 2: Pick 5 skills or qualities

With the selected extracurriculars in mind, consider all the skills and qualities you have shown and developed when undertaking these activities. Select <u>five</u> of these skills that you are most confident in discussing and illustrate your best qualities.

Example

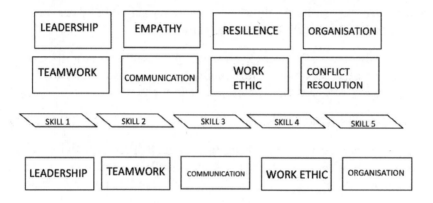

Step 3: Link achievements to skills

Review the extracurricular activities selected in Step 1 and assign the relevant skills that are demonstrated by each particular undertaking. Link together the skills and activities to form a list.

Example

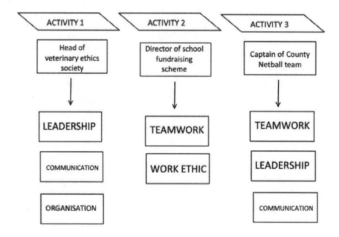

Step 4: Pick one activity per skill

The next step is to narrow down the list, such that each skill is assigned to just one activity. The objective of this step is to ensure you are prepared for the discussion of any particular quality at the interview, and to have an example ready to put forward.

Example

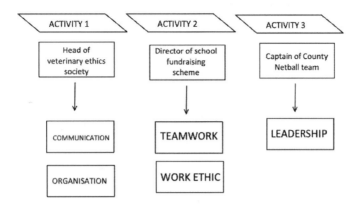

Step 5: Link back to medicine

Finally, link each skill back to medicine and explain the relevance to your future career. This can be achieved through discussing a scenario where you observed the skill being utilised during work experience. Alternatively, you may have ideas of how you will develop the skill over the course of your career and during medical school.

Example

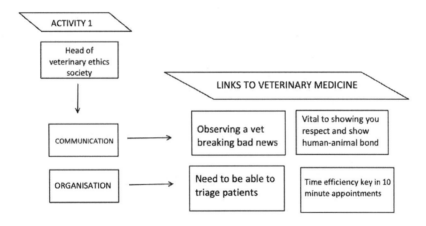

Sample responses

What is your greatest strength?

"I believe that I work well as a leader, so leadership is one of my strongest skills. As managing director of my young enterprise company, Derive, I developed the skills of delegation and management. I aim to be approachable to my team members, and work hard to lead by example. This will serve me well as a vet, a career in which I may manage teams in lots of settings."

Feedback

By using the Medic Mind framework this student has prepared for this question prior to the interview. The candidate is able to select a strong skill of their choice, describe a scenario that demonstrates and explain how this will be useful in their future career. The structure ensures all key elements are delivered succinctly.

Give three adjectives that best describe you.

"The first adjective I would use to describe myself is organised. Alongside studying for my A-Level exams, I have taken on multiple additional responsibilities such as Head of the animal welfare society over the past year. This required substantial organisation, to ensure smooth running of all society activities, alongside meeting academic deadlines and maintaining grades. Developing strong organisation skills is important for a career as a veterinarian, where prioritisation of tasks and patients is key. I would also describe myself using the adjectives leader and empathetic."

Feedback

This question invites candidates to discuss three skills of their choice. You may not have time to fully explore each skill and link it back to veterinary medicine. This answer opts to discuss organisation in full, and simply mentions leadership and empathy without discussing any achievements or links to veterinary medicine. It is important to be flexible with your approach in the context of strict time limits found in MMI stations.

4.2 Qualities of a vet

A career in veterinary medicine requires a host of specialised skills and knowledge. However, a successful vet will also possess many 'soft' skills in addition to their scientific knowledge. A 'soft' skill is one that often forms part of a person's personality and represents the qualities required to be able to appreciate the human-animal and demonstrate this between you (the vet) and your patient but also to respect and understand this bond between the patient and their client (pet and owner) in order to provide excellent care. Other skills required to be an excellent vet are non-technical skills that relate to the way you work, such as interactions with colleagues and managing a heavy workload. Vet school applicants should expect for certain elements of their personality to be assessed during an interview, as these qualities affect interactions with everyone from patients, to colleagues, to a patient's owners/clients.

Important qualities of a vet

The number of skills required in a vet is far-reaching, but common examples include:

- Teamwork
- Leadership
- Communication
- Organisation
- Empathy
- Compassion
- Scientific knowledge
- Manual dexterity
- Calmness

Applicants to veterinary schools should expect to be asked questions about skills more generally, such as *"What is the most important skill a vet needs?"*, which requires reflection and recognition of the multiple qualities essential to practice veterinary medicine. Interviewers may also ask about specific skills, for example *"Why is good communication important?"*, and are looking for understanding of the importance of that specific skill and reflections on a candidate's own abilities within that domain.

Expert's Advice

When asking about skills and personality, an interviewer may not ask about work experience directly. However these questions are an excellent opportunity to incorporate reflections of good practice you have observed. Simply stating that teamwork is important will not score highly - instead, a good candidate will explain the importance of teamwork and contribute their own experiences to strengthen their answer.

Sample responses

What is more important as a veterinary surgeon - being intelligent or having empathy?

"Intelligence is a key attribute for a good veterinary surgeon. Practising veterinary medicine requires a deep understanding of the scientific processes occurring inside the body of animals seen in practice as well as knowledge of pathophysiology, anatomy and pharmacology. In addition, a career

in veterinary medicine requires constant learning as new advances are made and consequently the ability to adapt and carry out lifelong study is important.

However, veterinary also requires a high level of social intelligence, of which empathy is a key part. Overall I would say that while both intelligence and empathy are vital skills for any vet surgeon, in some regards intelligence could be viewed as more important. Veterinary medicine is a holistic art, and communicating with clients requires a comforting and reassuring manner - without this the client can not trust you to respect the human-animal bond they have with their pet who is your patient. My reasoning is that a vet who is extremely empathetic but without the required scientific knowledge, will not be able to reach the correct diagnoses or select an appropriate treatment required to help that patient."

Feedback

This is a good answer. The candidate explains the importance of both qualities, giving a balanced answer. The answer could additionally be strengthened by using examples from work experience or extracurricular activities that demonstrate the importance of either scientific knowledge or empathy in veterinary medicine. A strong element of this answer is a final conclusion that sums up their view and makes a decision without sitting on the fence.

Common Pitfall

It is important to recognise that there is often no wrong answer to questions like this. An equally good candidate may have been able to justify empathy as the final answer. Remember it is not the final answer that will score you marks - it is how you reason and reach your conclusions.

If you were on the admissions board at this school of veterinary medicine, what skills or qualities would look for in applicants?

Example 1

"There are many qualities to look for in future vets. There are some skills that you cannot learn so I would focus on identifying those innate caring skills. For example, communication skills, and the ability to adapt communication style between different groups. This requires a candidate to be able to recognise the communication needs of different groups. Unlike the core sciences, this is not something that can be taught in a lecture hall but is equally important for patient care."

Feedback

This is a poor answer. The candidate is only able to identify a single quality and does not reflect on their own experiences. They also suggest that soft skills, such as communication, cannot be taught. This is a dangerous statement - you might end up being interviewed by the lead communication skills lecturer so be very careful when making broad or generalised statements like this. Additionally this candidate repeats themselves a lot and 'waffles on' with no cohesive conclusion statement.

Example 2

"The admissions board is looking to select candidates that demonstrate the potential to develop into excellent vets including academic potential and the soft skills required for a career in veterinary medicine. Examples of the qualities I would be looking for include empathy, strong communication

skills, resilience and compassion. In addition, an important skill to assess is teamwork as I believe it to be central to the modern veterinary world.

During my work experience placement in small animal veterinary surgery, I unfortunately witnessed an example of poor communication. A client brought their pet cat in for a routine fleaing appointment from the vet nurse. The nurse needed advice and clarification from the veterinary surgeon about a problem with the course of treatment and sent them a virtual message. Unfortunately, key information was missed from the message and the veterinarian provided incorrect advice. Subsequently the patient and client returned to the clinic a week later after the cat had experienced bloody lesions due to excessive scratching- complications of the initial problem. This illustrated to me the importance of strong teamwork skills as, in this case, the failure of multi-disciplinary team members to work well together results in a poor outcome for the patient."

Feedback

This is a good answer. The candidate is able to identify suitable qualities for a veterinary student. Crucially, this answer explores one of these qualities in more depth by reflecting on a work experience scenario. With this question, be prepared for follow-up questions exploring your own abilities in whichever skills you have mentioned.

Practice MMI station

Station brief

What attributes do you have that will make you a good vet?

Good answer A good answer may include:

- Identification of multiple key qualities essential for veterinarians
- Acknowledgment that both 'hard' and 'soft' skills are important
- Reflection on work experience, giving an example of a situation where key skills were demonstrated by the professionals at work
- Demonstration of key skills being developed by the candidate through extracurricular activities

Poor answer A poor answer may include:

- Overemphasis on academic attributes and knowledge - remember that the purpose of vet school is to teach you the medical knowledge needed to become a vet! While academic aptitude is important, in-depth medical knowledge is not required of an applicant.
- Superficial descriptions rather than deep reflection on one's own abilities and skills.

4.3 Teamwork

Being a strong team player is vital as a vet. The healthcare sector requires individuals in different roles to work together in the patient's best interests. The multidisciplinary team will include other healthcare professionals, such as nurses and technicians, but also vets of varying specialties and seniority. Questions assessing teamwork ability, both in a leadership and team-player capacity, are among some of the most common vet school interview questions.

Common pitfall

Remember to put the Medic Mind framework into practice and incorporate the skill (teamwork) to an extracurricular activity you have undertaken, and finally explain how this is relevant to veterinary medicine.

Sample responses

What are some features of a good team player?

"A good team player will contribute to the overall success of the team in multiple different ways. A team player will not only recognise their own strengths but will recognise the key skills and strengths of others and support them to contribute their strong points. A team player needs to have good communication skills and be able to take direction from others. An example that illustrates this to me is my experience on the committee of the animal welfare and veterinary ethics society in my school. We had a task to organise a fundraising event. A committee member was particularly experienced in fundraising, however the president of the society failed to appreciate this and attempted to organise the event by themselves. By not appreciating the significant experience of a team member, the president made multiple mistakes, wasted time and was less efficient overall. "

Feedback

This is a good answer. The response gives a number of features of a good team player and uses an example to illustrate what a bad team player looks like. An excellent candidate would push this answer even further and describe features of their own personality that make them a good team player with ideas of how they plan to develop these skills.

Why is teamwork important?

Example 1

"Teamwork is important as it allows the different strengths of each individual team member to combine. This means activities can be completed more efficiently based on each team member's strengths. When I was in the animal welfare and veterinary ethics society school, my personal strengths were in design and marketing and consequently my role focused on designing posters and managing social media. Whereas other members of the team focused on accounts and finances, or liaising with staff members as this was their strength."

Feedback

This is a weak answer. The candidate gives a good reason for the importance of teamwork, and is able to evidence this with personal experience. However this answer falls short as the student does not link or reflect on the way in which teamwork is applicable to veterinary medicine or a career as a vet. The response would be significantly strengthened by suggesting ways in which the student will use their teamwork skills and strengths during vet school and beyond.

Example 2

"Teamwork is important in many areas of life, but it is particularly important in a veterinary healthcare setting. In order to be successful, veterinary healthcare workers must act as a team to utilise the different skills each member contributes. It is important to understand that, even as a senior vet, no single person will know everything about every possible illness. By working as a team, you are able to bounce off other people's strengths and skills to support each other to reach the best possible outcome for the patient.

I saw a good example of this during my work experience on a cardiology ward in a pet hospital. I noticed how each member of the team had a particular area of the patient's care that they focused on and were very knowledgeable about. For example, a surgeon who performed the operations, yet a specialised vet anaesthetist took care of the patient during the operation and vet nurses cared for the patient after the operation. This made me reflect on how important it is to recognise the boundaries of your own knowledge and be able to consult other team members in the future."

Feedback

This is a good answer. The student shows they recognise some of the benefits of working in a team. They evidence this with observation from work experience and attempt to apply the lessons learnt to their future practice. This answer explains the importance of recognising your own limitations.

Practice MMI station

Station brief

During your time at vet school you will have to work in small groups, both in tutorials and on rotations in later years.

Why do you think we incorporated a large amount of teamwork into our curriculum?

Good answer A good answer may include:

- Understanding of the role teams play within veterinary healthcare and the contribution of the multidisciplinary team. For example, during a surgical procedure there may be multiple surgeons, anaesthetists, nurses and specialised practitioners.
- Knowledge of the curriculum and how teamwork is incorporated at that vet school. The candidate should draw parallels with the group work during vet school and the expectations of a vet to be a team player.
- Evidence of good teamwork carried out by the applicant, either as a team member or a leader.
- Suggestions for how the candidate's skills may fit into teamwork during vet school.

Poor answer A poor answer may include:

- Focus on leadership. The days of vets giving orders to other vet healthcare workers are gone. Modern medicine requires vets to be equally talented team members and leaders depending on the situation.
- Not answering the question fully with reference to the use of teamwork in the curriculum. Some candidates may interpret this question to be asking the merits of teamwork in general and despite giving an excellent explanation, will fail to score points as they do not answer the specific question.

4.4 Leadership

A vet will often take on a leadership role within the healthcare team. While other healthcare professionals contribute valuable skills, a vet is typically the ultimate decision maker in a patient's care. A vet school interview will assess your leadership potential by asking your perception of the qualities of a great leader, and by also asking you to draw on previous experiences of acting as a leader.

Common pitfall
Leadership and teamwork questions are often asked together, perhaps even in the same MMI station. It is important to differentiate between the two as a strong vet will act as both a leader and team member depending on the scenario.

If you have spent time witnessing a surgery during work experience you will have observed firsthand how a surgeon takes control and leads the surgery. The surgical environment is a great example of both teamwork and leadership. Within the surgical team every member has a clearly defined and important role which is vital for success of the operation. However, it is the veterinary surgeon who directs the progress of the procedure and draws on the expertise of other team members when needed.

Sample responses

What are some features of a good leader?

"A leader needs to be many things. They need to be motivational, organised and able to delegate appropriately. However in my opinion the best leaders are those who foster an environment that allows team members to feel comfortable to voice opinions and raise concerns. By doing so, the leader invites criticism in a safe environment so that conflicts or problems within any particular group or project can be addressed quickly.

An example of great leadership I have observed is the coach of my netball team. She is firm in her expectations yet when issues have arisen, such as episodes of bullying, she listens non-judgmentally to team members which enables other issues to come to light. I have tried to mimic this in my own leadership roles. For example, last year I was elected Head Girl at my school and made the effort during speeches to let the other students know that I was available to talk to them if they were facing difficulties. I hope to carry forward that approachability and ability to listen in future leadership scenarios as a vet."

Feedback

This is an excellent answer. The student gives a handful of qualities seen in good leaders, but expands on one particular element (approachability) in detail. This answer shows reflection on a good leader from an extracurricular activity, but then demonstrates how the candidate has put what they have learnt into action in their own life.

Do you prefer working alone or in a team?

"Teamwork and independent working both come with their benefits and challenges. Through working as a group, you can collaborate and draw upon the individual strengths of each team member to work more efficiently. Teams also help you avoid errors and allow you to get a second opinion. For example, in a healthcare team a vet nurse is able to draw upon the knowledge of veterinary surgeons who can give advice for delegation tasks taken on by vet nurses.

Working alone also has some advantages such as a greater degree of independence and ability to direct your work. While my personal preference would be to work in a team, I am also comfortable working independently and understand that a vet must be able to do both in different settings. I know teamwork takes a central role in learning at this veterinary school, through directed learning (DL) teaching. The opportunity to work in a group for a significant part of my studies is something that attracted me to apply here."

Feedback

This is a good answer. The student is able to appreciate the benefits of both independent and group work, but is able to make a choice between the two and justify this. The inclusion of healthcare-related examples shows a degree of reflection on how teamwork fits into the work of a vet.

Expert's Advice

Remember that a question asking you to pick between two options often has no right or wrong answer. An interviewer is looking for a balanced answer and a reasonable justification for the option you decide. Try not to get caught up in which option to choose in the conclusion to your answer, instead focus on how to explore the reasoning behind that choice.

Practice MMI station

Station brief

You are working on a group project as part of the coursework during your degree. Team members are expected to contribute equally to the task.

Initially the project was going well but now one particular member of the group, Layla, has stopped attending group meetings and is not meeting deadlines relevant to her parts. This has gone on for several weeks and is negatively impacting your progress as a group.

As the group leader, how would you approach this situation?

Good answer A good answer may include:

- Awareness of some of the reasons a student may withdraw from a group task such as illness, stress and burnout.
- Approaching Layla with compassion and empathy. A good leader is non-judgemental and sensitive to group members experiencing difficulties
- Escalating to staff only if unable to resolve the issue within the group, or if Layla reveals a serious reason underlying her absence and requires external help.
- Provides pragmatic solutions or strategies to support Layla.

Poor answer A poor answer may include:

- Reporting or consulting to staff members directly. As a leader you should try and resolve the problem yourself first, especially as it is not too serious.
- Being overly confrontational. Empathy is an important quality and you should consider why Layla has changed her behaviour recently.
- Generates friction within the group by involving other group members and drawing attention to Layla's lack of contribution.

4.5 Empathy

Veterinary medicine is often regarded as being both an art and a science - your biomedical knowledge of the workings of the animal body is applied in a holistic approach taking into account the social and emotional needs of that individual patient as well as any people involved with this patient. Empathy is definitely something of a buzzword for vet school interviews and will certainly be assessed in some shape or form. However, ensure you fully understand the meaning of empathy and the important role it plays in a veterinary medicine setting.

Empathy and sympathy

The distinction between empathy and sympathy is a common topic in vet school interviews. These two concepts are very similar, but it is important to feel confident clearly explaining the differences.

Common Pitfall

Some candidates fall into the trap of using empathy and sympathy interchangeably. While the difference between the two terms can appear subtle at first, there is a key distinction to understand. Both terms relate to ways of handling emotions in difficult situations, but empathy is a much deeper response.

Both empathy and sympathy are useful in different situations. Empathy refers to the ability to share the feelings of another. In other words, empathy is putting yourself in another person's shoes to experience their emotions and understanding their point of view. On the other hand, sympathy describes the feeling of pity or sorrow for another person. In veterinary medicine, sympathy for clients can come across as patronising, regardless of how well-meaning, so it is better avoided. Empathy promotes a connection between client and vet due to your empathy being the basis of understanding their human-animal bond, whereas sympathy fuels disconnection.

Consider the situation where a patient is in hospital and experiencing severe pain. The phrase *"I am sorry this is happening to your pet"* directed to their owner suggests that the speaker does not share the patient's experience of seeing their beloved pet in pain. This lends to the tendency to "talk down" and creates a division between the person who is suffering and the person who is not. Whereas the alternative phrase *"I can see that things must be very hard for you right now"* shows empathy as the speaker has imagined what it is like to be the client, and validated their experience. They are understanding of the problem and, even though the pain is not physically shared, they are accepting without making the problem about themselves.

Sample responses

What does the word empathy mean to you?

"Empathy describes the experience of putting yourself in someone else's shoes and understanding their point of view. Without empathy a vet would not understand the experiences of our clients who bring in our patients and may ignore or be ignorant to factors important to their care. By showing empathy, a client is more likely to feel an emotional connection to their vet and this may prompt them to disclose sensitive information, or follow   the   vet's   advice.

During my work experience I can remember a particular moment where the vet displayed immense empathy. A client brought their dog in who was suffering with cancer, the client did not want to go ahead with any clinic treatment but instead wanted advice on a more holistic approach. Instead of being paternalistic or disapproving, the vet was non-judgemental and asked the client to share her concerns with the clinical approach. Even though the vet did not personally share the views of the client, she validated her concerns by empathising that any pet owner would be concerned about the risks of a medical intervention. By doing this, the vet was able to gently challenge the client without causing a confrontation. "

Feedback

As with all questions about personal qualities, make sure to link the answer back to veterinary medicine and why it is relevant for a career as a vet. This answer could have been strengthened by deeper reflection by exploring how the student plans to use empathy in their future studies or career.

Are you an empathetic person?

"Empathy is a key skill for vets, and all members of the veterinary healthcare team. As a vet it is important to show empathy to your clients in order to strengthen the vet-patient relationship as well as the human-animal bond between vet and patient. I believe myself to be an empathetic person. For example, over the past year I have been volunteering in a care home on the weekends. My role involves helping out with activities and facilitating socialisation between the residents.

During one session, a resident began to tell me about the death of her husband and became visibly upset. I made a cup of tea for us both and sat down in a quiet area with her. I displayed empathy by acknowledging her sorrow and encouraging her to share her memories if she felt comfortable. It was heartening for me at the end of the day when she expressed her gratitude for my kindness."

Feedback

This answer gives a good answer of a time where the candidate demonstrated empathy. The first paragraph links the skill to veterinary medicine and shows an understanding of why empathy is important within veterinary healthcare.

Common Pitfall

This question focuses on you and is asking for you to share your own experience of empathy. Some candidates fail to recognise this and instead may reflect on a time they witnessed empathy during their work experience. This does not show the interviewer how they themselves are empathetic and consequently will not score highly. If a question asks about you specifically, make sure you use examples where you have directly contributed.

Practice MMI stations

Station brief

This station will focus on exploring your personal qualities and how these make you suitable to become a vet.

As a vet you will have to break bad news and deal with situations where things go wrong. How will you cope with this emotionally?

Good answer A good answer may:

- Understand the importance of relating to a client when breaking bad news. We need to show empathy to avoid being overly cold or clinical.
- A good candidate will also avoid being overly emotional. There is a balance between being too corporate and too sentimental. Healthcare professionals need to keep an emotional distance in order to think properly and behave appropriately.
- Reference any work experience or volunteering. Reflection on observations of difficult situations or describing how a candidate has developed their own communication skills would strengthen an answer.

Poor answer A poor answer may:

- Admit that this is an area where the candidate would struggle. A surprising number of candidates respond to this question by saying they are emotional and will find breaking bad news too challenging.
- Being apathetic. Some candidates say they would approach difficult situations by being fully unemotional and detached, treating the patient as a scientific case.

Station brief

You are a third year veterinary medicine student studying for your exams. Your friend, Simon, asks to meet with you after a particularly long and stressful day on placement. He tells you he cannot cope with life at vet school and wishes to drop out to go travelling instead. He is asking for your advice on how to communicate this decision to his parents.

Notes for actor (Simon)

You are feeling incredibly anxious for the upcoming third year exams. You have not started revision and can not find the motivation to do so. Your parents have always wanted you to become a vet and the weight of their expectations plays on your mind a lot. Your main worry is failing your exams and disappointing your parents in this way.

Good answer A good answer will:

- Use active listening skills to fully explore Simon's point of view and the factors leading up to his decision to leave vet school.
- Use empathetic phrases to encourage Simon to open up, for example *"I can see that you're struggling at the moment"* or *"This must be a very difficult situation"*.

Poor answer A poor answer will include:

- Judgmental views or immediately persuading Simon to stay. Without knowing Simon's background we cannot know if dropping out of vet school is the right thing for him to do. Although studying veterinary medicine may be the correct career path for the candidate, we cannot assume this is true for Simon too.

- Quick attempts to fix the problem without fully understanding Simon's point of view. Often being empathetic is less about solving the issue, but listening and encouraging the other person to find their own solutions.
- Sympathetic phrases rather than empathetic. Try to avoid inserting your own views or experiences into your responses. This conversation should be about Simon and his experience.

4.6 Organisation

During vet school and throughout a career in veterinary medicine, it is vital to remain organised and on top of the vast amount of work given. If you have spent time in a small animal practice during work experience you will have observed the multitude of different tasks the GP is required to perform in short 10 minute appointment slots. Even while at vet school, students need to be able to balance the demands of studying alongside attending placements, maintaining a social life and taking part in hobbies.

Prioritisation and learning to make decisions depending on the urgency of different tasks is crucial to efficient working. A patient with a life threatening condition needs to be seen sooner than a patient with a minor ailment. These prioritisation skills, or 'triaging' can be applied to studying too. For example, a student who focuses on revising for an imminent exam rather than a piece of coursework that is not due until the following month is more likely to be successful. In this chapter we will discuss various organisation skills and questions regarding a student's ability to manage their time.

Time management strategies

It is useful to have a number of time management strategies prepared to use in relevant questions. These could be examples of organisation skills you already employ to manage your school work, or plans to avoid burnout. You do not need to mention every possible organisation skill or strategy. Incorporate the methods that are relevant to you and for which you would genuinely use in your further studies.

Keeping a diary

One of the most simple but effective time management strategies is using a diary or planner. This allows you to keep track of deadlines and other important events in your schedule. You could even use a digital calendar or note-taking app for the same purpose.

Prioritisation of tasks

Being able to focus your attention on the tasks that are most important is a critical skill to learn. The ability to identify the most urgent areas of work is a skill that should not be underestimated. Strategies enabling prioritisation include constructing a prioritisation matrix or delegating less important tasks.

De-stress

A career in veterinary medicine is often stressful and it is important to have strategies in place to avoid burnout. Vet schools are keen to see students recognising their own limitations and understanding the importance of a life outside of veterinary medicine. Your de-stress techniques do not have to be sophisticated and may be as simple as doing exercise or spending time with loved ones.

Making a list of tasks

Constructing a to-do list is the fundamental basis of most organisation techniques. If you spent time in a hospital during work experience you may have noticed final year vet students constructing a 'jobs list' during the morning ward round. Writing a to-do list also facilitates prioritisation and planning ahead. For example, you may have lists for immediate tasks to be completed today as well as lists for the near and distant future.

Planning ahead

Having an idea of upcoming tasks and events will allow you to plan accordingly. Veterinary medicine is a broad subject and during your time at vet school you are expected to learn an enormous amount of content. Leaving an entire module's worth of content to revise at the last minute is not an efficient strategy. Rather, planning ahead and ensuring you have sufficient time to fully cover the content is more favourable. Examples of this strategy that you could mention include constructing a revision timetable and allocating tasks to certain be completed in specific time frames.

Balancing time

While it is helpful to plan ahead, remember to be flexible and allow for adjustments to your schedule too. The life of a vet is unpredictable and sometimes you will need to change plans with very short notice. By incorporating a degree of flexibility into your organisation plans, a candidate demonstrates a realistic expectation of their career to the interviewers.

Common Pitfall

When discussing organisation during a vet school interview, always give a solution as part of your answer. Instead of simply saying you will balance your time, instead use examples of the methods you plan to employ to do so.

Sample responses

Tell me about a non-academic project in which you were involved.

"Over the past year I have held the position of Fundraising Lead for my sixth form. This role required me to organise all the fundraising activities in our school to support our chosen charities. The role was busy and involved managing a team of six students of varying ages as well as liaising with staff members and various charitable departments. This required a great deal of organisation to manage alongside revising for my A-Levels. For example, when arranging a particular event I realised that it would clash with some of my exams. To manage this I constructed a to-do list and prioritised the most important tasks that could be completed in advance. This allowed me to optimise the use of my time, while also leaving time to revise. Time management is an important skill for studying at vet school, as well as a career in veterinary medicine, and I hope to apply the skills I learned as a Fundraising Lead to my future studies."

Feedback

This question is not specifically asking about organisation or time management skills, but is a good opportunity to demonstrate them. The candidate could have equally chosen to use this question to demonstrate empathy, leadership or other key skills.

How do you plan to stay organised during your time at our vet school?

"To manage my time I ensure that I make lists to plan tasks, I prioritise in order of urgency for tasks, I use contingencies to account for tasks taking long and I take plenty of time to relax to destress. I also keep an up-to-date   calendar."

Feedback

This candidate has given some good strategies for remaining organised during vet school. However the answer fails to provide any evidence of further insight or explanation, and instead simply provides a list. Ensure that every point, or strategy, you mention in an answer is fully expanded. It is far better to take one or two points and fully explore them, than to simply list a larger number of points.

"Organising myself is something I am used to from school. This year, I had to manage and organise my time effectively to ensure that I could participate in my charity fundraising team alongside my school work. To do this, I allocated set times to do my school work, and also made lists to ensure that I was aware of what had to be done. Of course, I also left time to relax, ensuring that when I did work I did so efficiently."

Feedback

This is a stronger answer. The student uses examples from their charity work to illustrate clear examples using their chosen strategies in action. The final sentence mentions the importance of relaxing and leaving time to de-stress. This is a good way to finish the answer as it communicates to the interviewer that this candidate understands the importance of recreation and is unlikely to overwork themselves.

Practice MMI station

Station brief

Veterinary medicine involves a great deal of independent study. How will you manage it?

Good answer A good answer may include:

- Understanding of the different activities a vet student undertakes in independent study e.g. placements, preparing for dissection sessions and lectures.
- Reflection on own limitations and appropriate strategies to remain organised given the workload of a vet degree.
- Examples of time management for independent projects from previous projects or studies.
- Highlighting the importance of downtime to 'recharge' in order to remain efficient and avoid burnout.

Poor answer A poor answer may include:

- Dismissal or attempts to minimise the demands of a vet degree on students.
- Providing a list of organisation strategies without applying this to a veterinary context or explanation of how these would help the student.
- Admitting that organisation is a personal struggle and that it will be hard to manage independent studying alongside the demands of a vet degree.

Practice MMI station
Station brief

A cat has just been brought into your clinic after having just been hit by a car. You do not know who the owner is or any other history about the cat but you noticed the cat is profusely bleeding from the mouth, struggling to breath and is panting, has a high temperature, is crying in pain and you noticed the cat also has a   quite   severe   flea   infestation.

Please rank the following clinical signs in order of most important to least important:

- High temperature
- Panting
- Flea infestation
- Bleeding from mouth
- Crying in pain

Answer:

- Panting
- Bleeding from mouth
- Crying in pain
- High temperature
- Flea infestation

For this prioritisation station there are two emergencies : panting and breathing from the mouth. As long as you state that both of these are emergencies during your reasoning you will be scored highly. A good candidate may even link these two emergencies for example by saying how the bleeding is causing lack of oxygen which is causing the panging. This shows to the interviewer you have knowledge of how the cardiovascular and respiratory systems are necessary for life.

Good answer In a good answer, you would:

- **Recognise the life-threatening clinical signs -** Prioritise these first.
- **Show good understanding of how they can fix the problem -** If you can go into detail about how you can fix these or why you have placed them first this would show good understanding. Ie if the cat is struggling to breathe putting it on oxygen or in an oxygen chamber for a few minutes to stabilise it would be a good suggestion.
- **Think smart -** If you can, try to see if there is a link between the clinical signs here, or decide whether the cat has multiple problems. E.g. increased temperature, is the cat hot or is it warm because it is stressed and has been panting?

Poor answer In a poor answer, you might:

- **Prioritise the flea infestation before anything else -** This is definitely not the most important issue here and it is likely the animal has had fleas for a long time.
- **Not recognize the cat is in pain and address this.**
- **Spend more time trying to work out what exactly happened to the cat before prioritising what is wrong with it -** This is not important right now and if the cat is not stabilised soon it will die. You can always find out details later.
- **Not recognize the severity of the bleeding -** In this scenario it does not state how badly the cat is bleeding, but good candidates will want to question this and will know that severe, profuse bleeding has more consequences than if the cat has just scuffed its face.

4.7 Strengths and Weaknesses

In previous chapters we have discussed the approach to questions addressing specific skills such as teamwork, leadership and empathy. However, some questions are broader and ask candidates to self-identify areas of strength or weakness in their own personality. It is easy to over complicate such questions, as candidates are keen to hide or shield negative or weaker aspects of their character.

Biggest weakness

A common vet school interview question asks candidates to discuss their biggest weakness. Interviewers are looking for students to identify a genuine weakness and to have taken initiative to take steps to improve. The skill of reflection is critical in the development of a good vet, and all vets are required to reflect on their own abilities throughout their career. Vet school interviewers are keen to identify candidates who already reflect on their own skills and have acted upon this.

Step 1: Introduction

The first step to answering a question about your biggest weakness is to provide a short introduction and set the scene to your answer. You should recognise the fact that everyone, no matter how skilled, will have a relative weakness alongside their strengths. Identifying weaknesses is critical for self-development and should not be shied away from.

Step 2: Identify a weakness

The choice of weakness that you discuss is important. Take the time to reflect on your personality and pick a **genuine** weakness to discuss. Try to avoid cliché responses including perfectionism as a negative quality.

Expert's Advice

When discussing a personal weakness try and use the past tense where the question allows. This emphasises to the interviewers that you have since developed and improved the skill from the point in time that you identified it as a weakness.

Step 3: Discuss the process of development

After recognising a weakness, you should aim to illustrate the steps taken to progress and develop that specific area or skill. This may include talking to teachers, asking for feedback, watching tutorials or reading articles to learn improvement methods. Detail the steps you took and how these have helped you.

Step 4: Show positivity

Finally, frame the discussion in a positive light and turn the initial weakness into a current strength. Acknowledge that, while it has taken effort to improve, because of your efforts the skill that was once a struggle is now a personal asset. Illustrate this by using an example where you have used that particular skill and thrived doing so.

Sample responses

"I tend to be quite bad with my decision making, for example I underestimate the time taken to complete a task. In the past this has led me to take on too many tasks and I have struggled to complete them as I run out of time."

Feedback

This is a poor answer. The student is overly negative about their weakness and this may lead the admissions panel to conclude that they would struggle with the demands of a medical course. The student could avoid this by adding examples of how they have developed or overcome their weak decision making skills.

"I can sometimes manage my time too ambitiously meaning I take on too many responsibilities which in turn leads to stress. For example, last year I took part in the school enterprise scheme, played rugby and ran my school's veterinary ethics society. I ended up not having enough time to enjoy my time in each role and I spread myself too thin."

Feedback

The weakness selected by this candidate is a good choice. It comes across as genuine and the student is able to give an example. However, this answer fails to provide evidence of improvement. The student should discuss how they went about improving their difficulties with time management and the ways in which they are better now.

"My biggest weakness is my tendency to underestimate how long tasks will take me. In the past this has led me to taking on too many responsibilities which has resulted in increased stress. For example, during Year 11 I was Head Boy at school, played rugby at county level, took part in the Young Enterprise scheme and ran my school's veterinary ethics society. I found myself being spread too thin and I was conscious of the impact it may have on my academics. To counter this I had a discussion with my Head of Year about my difficulties. He was very helpful and helped me to delegate some of responsibility and prioritise the most important tasks. Now, I make sure to schedule my time in advance and avoid taking on more tasks than I can manage to ensure I remain organised."

Feedback

This is a much stronger answer. The student clearly details the steps they took to address their weakness. As a result the student comes across as proactive and showing initiative.

Talking about strengths

An interviewer may ask you to describe your greatest strengths or attributes. These questions are far easier to answer compared to questions about weaknesses. The interviewer is looking for you to identify an appropriate, realistic strength aligned to a career in veterinary medicine. The best way to do this is to talk about skills to fully develop your answer and relate it to veterinary medicine.

Practice MMI station

Station brief

Describe a time where you made a mistake.

Good   answer   A   good   answer   may   include:

- Genuine, true and realistic example of a suitable mistake.
- A positive approach, describing how the candidate used lessons from the mistake to improve themselves after reflecting on it.

Poor answer A poor answer may include:

- Description of a mistake that questions the candidate's suitability or professionalism, such as cheating on an exam.
- Overly negative or apologetic language without a focus on reflection and learning from the mistake.

4.8 Practice Questions: Personal Qualities & Skills

1. Why should we give you a place at our vet school?
2. What attributes do you have that will make you a good vet?
3. Could you think of a situation where your communication skills made a difference to the outcome of a situation?
4. Are you an empathetic person?
5. Who has had a major influence on you as a person?
6. Give an example where you have played an effective role as a team member.
7. What makes you a good team player?
8. What makes you a good team leader?
9. Why is teamwork important in healthcare?
10. Do all teams need a leader?
11. What are the advantages and disadvantages of working in a team?
12. Are you a leader or a follower?
13. How do you manage your time?
14. What is the difference between empathy and sympathy?
15. How do you tackle criticism?
16. How would you give another vet student criticism?
17. How do you plan to overcome the challenges of veterinary medicine?
18. What personal qualities do you think you need to improve in order to be a better vet?
19. How do you think other people describe you?
20. How would you cope with the death of a patient?
21. When do you seek out help with your academics?
22. Do you consider yourself a perfectionist? Why or why not?
23. Do you think academic or social intelligence is more important as a vet?
24. What positions of responsibility have you held, and what did you learn from them?
25. Give an example of a situation where you have made a mistake and how you acted.
26. What is/was your favourite subject to study at school?
27. Give an example of a time where you showed resilience.
28. How do you tackle conflict?
29. Give an example of when you displayed good communication skills.
30. Do you think communication skills can be taught?
31. What skills are most important in a vet?
32. Why is professionalism important in veterinary medicine?
33. Give an example of something that you had a strong opinion on but you changed your mind. What made you change your mind? What do you think now?
34. What do you think will be your greatest challenge in veterinary medicine?
35. Describe an event that you planned. Was it successful? How would you improve it?
36. Do you think vets should "feel for their patients and clients"?
37. What would you do if you were unsure of a patient's diagnosis?
38. What element of your personality would you like to change?
39. Why do you think you would be a good vet?
40. What strengths would you bring to your group in a problem-based learning session?

1:1 VET INTERVIEW TUTORING

 Delivered by current Vet students, who have excelled in the interview themselves

 A personalised 1:1 approach, tailored to your unique needs

 Learn how to answer questions on motivation, skills, work experience, veterinary ethics, anatomy, and more

EXCLUSIVE OFFER: GET 70% OFF YOUR FIRST LESSON

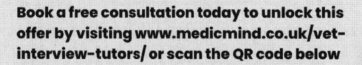

Book a free consultation today to unlock this offer by visiting www.medicmind.co.uk/vet-interview-tutors/ or scan the QR code below

VET INTERVIEW ONLINE COURSE

 Video tutorials, designed by our Vet interview experts, to guide you through the most common question topics

 Top tips and techniques to construct the perfect interview answers under time pressure

 Model answers and practice questions to aid you in your preparation

EXCLUSIVE OFFER: GET 10% OFF USING THE CODE BOOK10

Find out more at www.medicmind.co.uk/veterinary-medicine-interview-online-course-2023/ or scan the QR code below

CHAPTER 5

V Knowing the veterinary school

5.1 Introduction

When you study veterinary medicine you are committing yourself to studying at a particular vet school for a period of several years. Universities are looking for you to have made an informed decision about not just becoming a vet b ut also your choice of vet school. This means you are expected to have some degree of knowledge of each vet course and the teaching that is offered.

Common Pitfall

Prospective veterinary applicants are often guided to make 'strategic applications', by applying to schools they think they are most likely to receive an offer from. Admissions panels will not see this as an acceptable reason for submitting an application. You should avoid any mention of statistics or the probability of success in your answers.

Talking about veterinary courses

Course structure

Research the course structure and use this to answer questions about that specific vet school. Some of the points that could be raised when discussing each vet school are listed below.

Placement locations

During your vet degree you will undertake placements at various different hospitals, farms, stables and clinics. The geographical area covered by each vet school can be quite varied and include some interesting placements. Most vet schools in the UK have two campuses, one in a city area and one in a more rural area on the outskirts of the city for farm and hospital placements. So consider how close these two campuses are to each other and make sure you like both locations.

Hospital specialisms

Some vet schools are affiliated with specialist hospitals or specialist sites . For example, students at Bristol vet school have an opportunity to visit Langfords onsite abattoir. It is a good idea to research the vet school's main hospitals along with other facilities they have(such as equine referral units, abattoirs etc) and take note of any unique or interesting departments that tie into your own interests.

Clinical academic mix

Most vet schools require students to dedicate their first 2 years of their course to pre-clinic theory academic work which then leads onto the final 3 years based at a different campus dedicated to clinical work. Here you will be doing more animal handling. However studying veterinary medicine at Cambridge means you will dedicate 3 years to pre-clinical learning and 3 years to clinical learning.

Other opportunities

 Vet school offers students a wealth of opportunities beyond acquiring a vet degree. Some universities offer the opportunity to study an intercalated degree, meaning students can obtain an additional qualification in an area   of   interest   at   BSc   or   Masters   level.   Intercalation   can   be   compulsory or optional depending on the vet school. Intercalation allows students to direct and shape their studies according to personal interests with RVC offering a popular pathology course. If you have a particular passion or are excited to explore a specific area of veterinary medicine, mentioning this in the context of these opportunities will show you have thought about your future at that vet school.

Expert's Advice

Pay careful attention to how the vet school markets themselves. Carefully read the website or any other promotional information and take note of the key selling points that they have chosen to highlight. These points are likely the areas of the course that the vet school thinks are the most attractive. Try to incorporate these points into your answers where possible.

5.2 Teaching Styles

You may have noticed that there are differences in the teaching styles offered across vet schools. Before your interview make sure to research the vet school's syllabus and find out about the type of course they offer.

It is very common to be asked about the vet school's curriculum in your interview. It is expected that consideration of teaching style will have been a key factor in your decision to apply to that particular vet school. The interviewers are looking for you to be knowledgeable about their curriculum and to demonstrate that you are well suited to the style of teaching.

Common Pitfall

Remember to explain to the interviewer why your skills complement the curriculum. You need to convince the panel their teaching style is well fitting to you. Avoid simply listing elements of the curriculum without explaining why each aspect would benefit your learning overall.

Spiral/strand learning

Spiral or strand learning is common in a lot of vet schools given the preclinical to clinical year learning difference. It refers to learning the basics for one subject (for example locomotor) in year 1, then developing more on that and only revisiting it in year 2. You will then revisit it in years 3-4 where you will learn what can go wrong with locomotion and how this can be resolved clinically.

An advantage of strand based learning is that you are not overwhelmed with too much information at one given time. Strand based learning allows vet students to constantly be referring and integrating their theory knowledge into clinical settings in later years up until actual vet work post graduation.

Sample responses

Why do you want to study a strand/spiral learning course?

"I assume that strand or spiral learning will provide a small amount of learning that is only necessary for that year which will really help me. I sometimes struggle to concentrate when given too much information to revise so I think I will be more suited to a building on learning approach."

<u>Feedback</u>

This answer is too negative. The candidate places too much emphasis on why this learning would **not** suit them rather than why it **will** suit their learning style. This may lead the interviewer to question if the student would struggle to cope with the demands of the course.

"I find integration and applying work extremely rewarding as I feel that I am better suited to learn by understanding how what I have learnt applies to clinical practice. This is because I find it much more engaging and interactive compared to learning a large scale of information all at once"

Feedback

This answer uses the same key points but is framed more positively. The student focuses on the aspects of strand learning where they would thrive. This comes across as more positive and optimistic than the previous answer, and as a result the student appears enthusiastic and self-motivated.

Expert's Advice

As with other types of questions, try and use examples from previous studies to provide evidence for your main points. For example, reflecting on a school group project where you performed well and drawing comparisons to a strand learning session will help convince the admissions panel you are well suited to their curriculum.

Rotations

During your 4th year and into 5th year you will be placed into small groups - this is your rotation group. During rotations, you and your group will work together as a team during clinical rounds in different settings such as hospitals or on farms.

Your rotation group is a good way to apply how you should be working in a team as you will eventually be doing this once a practising vet.

Why do you think the course at this vet school suits you?

"After reading your prospectus, I read up more about how rotations work in the final years of vet school. I really feel this will benefit me as I like to work in a team. I wasn't sure how I would deal with being independent in a clinical setting so decided to apply for a rotation based course as it seems like a good way to gain more confidence."

Feedback

 This is a poor answer. The student comes across as unsure and uncommitted to the vet school. There is little reflection on their own skills or learning style, and this does little to convince the interviewer that they would be a good fit for their vet school.

"I really like how the course here prides itself on team based learning in a clinical setting, which means that I will benefit from being a leader and independent studies but also gain the benefits of natural teamworking skills. This will enable me to gain a variety of skills including engaging in peer-learning problem solving seen in clinical practice. I tend to prefer independent study at school and I am looking forward to trying out new ways seen and valued specifically in practice to be able to become the best vet possible."

Feedback

This is a better answer. The student has clearly researched the course and comes across as excited and enthusiastic. They also demonstrate a degree of reflection through the recognition of how an integrated learning style will enable the development of relevant skills needed to work in a team.

Other styles of learning

Vet schools are constantly updating their curriculum and new teaching styles are emerging each year. For example, in recent years some universities have introduced blended learning referring to lectures done in one's own time alongside in person scheduled lecturers.

Regardless of the teaching style, remember to thoroughly research the course structure and prepare a handful of key benefits ready to discuss at interview. You should do this for each individual vet school and be specific to each course.

5.3 Dissection and Prosection

Anatomy is taught during the preclinical phase of a veterinary degree. The topic of anatomy is taught in a variety of ways with a surprising amount of variation in teaching methods between UK vet schools. Anatomy is traditionally one of the toughest aspects of veterinary medicine for first-year students, so it is worth researching the teaching at your chosen universities before attending an interview.

Expert's Advice

Although some interviews will assess you on basic anatomy knowledge, understanding of anatomy teaching is not a topic that needs to be brought up at every vet school interview. Only mention it if this is an area you are particularly interested in, or if the vet school you are applying to has an interesting approach to teaching.

Dissection

Cadaveric dissection is the traditional method of teaching anatomy to vet students. It involves cutting a body specimen to reveal anatomical structures to aid learning. Vet schools utilising dissection will expect students to carry out the dissection themselves, often in small groups, using animal cadavers.

Dissection is a very hands-on approach and allows students to see, physically touch, and explore organs to further their learning.

Prosection

In contrast to traditional dissection, prosection involves students examining pre-prepared cadaveric samples. This means all of the cutting and dissection is performed by trained anatomists instead of students themselves. The major advantage of this is the high quality of dissection which can make it easier to identify important structures.

Prosection is becoming increasingly favoured by vet schools, as it is a more time efficient method of teaching. Students also have the opportunity to examine samples from multiple cadavers and can more easily gain an appreciation of normal anatomical variations.

Sample responses

Do you think you will find cadaveric dissection useful?

"To be honest, I am scared of blood and so feel a bit nervous about having to see dead animals but I will try my best to overcome my fears. I also don't think that working with cadavers will be useful as vets operate on living patients and not ones that have already died."

Feedback

This is a poor answer. The student fails to appreciate the unique learning experience that dissection could provide. This leaves a negative and uninterested impression on the interviewer.

"Yes of course! I am a visual learner and find that reinforcing something I read in a textbook into a real-life example will enable me to consolidate information better. I also feel it provides a far better reflection of the complexity of the specimen body than drawn-diagrams do, as they represent an accurate representation of anatomical knowledge."

Feedback

This student is enthusiastic and shows the interviewer they have reflected on dissection and can see benefits for their learning. The answer is positive and focuses on the strengths of dissection.

5.4 Practice Questions: Knowing the vet school

1. What interests you about the curriculum at this university?
2. How does this vet school differ from the other schools you have applied to?
3. Tell me about the course we offer here.
4. Do you know much about the city this university is located in?
5. How do you learn best?
6. Are there any aspects of the course that you are particularly looking forward to?
7. Are there any aspects of the course that you are not looking forward to?
8. Why do you think we chose a traditional curriculum of preclinical and clinical years?
9. Why did you apply here?
10. How did you decide which vet schools to apply to?
11. Would you prefer rotations in a small animal clinic or a large teaching hospital?
12. Apart from studying the vet course, are there any aspects of university life that you're looking forward to?
13. How do you think teaching will be different at university compared to at school?
14. If you had to redesign the veterinary medicine curriculum how would you do it?
15. Why would a traditional teaching style suit you?
16. Why does the location of this university appeal to you?
17. What are the advantages of attending this particular vet school?
18. What are the disadvantages of attending this particular vet school?
19. How much do you know about dissection?
20. How much do you know about prosection?
21. Would you rather learn anatomy through dissection or prosection?
22. If you were designing a vet degree, at what stage would you introduce clinical placements and animal handling opportunities?
23. Would you want to undertake an intercalated degree?
24. What are the benefits of studying veterinary as a graduate?
25. How would you contribute to our vet school's community?
26. What does it mean when we describe our course as 'integrated'?
27. What are the benefits of a foundation year before veterinary medicine?

CHAPTER 6

VI Anatomy MMI

6.1 Introduction

As it is a crucial role to your study and your career as a vet, during your interview you will more than likely be tested on your knowledge of anatomy. This could be in the form of a picture, a model, Skeleton or a cadaver pot. The actual anatomy you may be tested on varies between stations so make sure you have a basic baseline knowledge of anatomy

In this station you will be asked to describe what you see, you will then be asked further questions relating to the structure or complications involved with the subject at hand.

Preparing

Although it might sound counterintuitive, having a basic understanding of human anatomy will aid you in this part of your vet interview. It is much easier to relate to your own body when trying to grasp learning anatomy which you can then apply to different animals who have slightly different anatomy to humans.

This is also beneficial as a common station for MMI anatomy is to compare two different animal skeletons. So by understanding and thinking of comparative anatomy you are on the way to giving a good answer.

Don't just think about bones! Not all anatomy is at large scale. The station you are faced with in your MMI may be an histology slide of a cell. So make sure when researching and thinking about this station you consider organs and cells which you may have come across in A-level biology.

6.2 How should I approach anatomy questions?

Here is a list of questions that you can use when revising for interviews to help you solve anatomy stations.

1.   Is there any structure in the human that is comparable to this?

2.   What is the function of this structure in the animal and in the human?

3.   How does this structure work in the human and in the animal?

4.   Why might this animal have/ have not evolved this structure?

5.   Why might we as humans have evolved/ have not evolved this structure?

6.   Are there any differences in the way that the animal uses the structure compared to a human?

If you can ask yourself these 6 questions when faced with an anatomy question they will help you to think outside of the box in order to help to try and identify the structure... even if you do not know what it is!

Expert's Advice

If you truly have no clue what the anatomy is you are being shown do not panic. You will more than likely know at least one structure in what is being shown to you so draw on that and the interviewer will guide the question on this so you are able to talk about it. If you are still unsure, guess ! This station is more about your thought process rather than you regurgitating an anatomy book.

Practice MMI station

Station brief

Please look at the following image and answer the following questions:

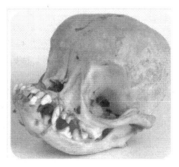

1.   What is the structure in the photo?

2.   Why   do   you   think   that   it   is   this   structure?

3.   Can you guess what breed this structure is from?

4.   Why do you think this?

5.   How might this structure cause health problems compared to a 'normal' structure of this?

Answer

1.   The structure in the photo is a skull from a dog.

2.   The teeth look like from a carnivorous animal, eyes on the front of the head suggest this animal is a predator species (for dogs this is from their distant relatives the wolf).

3.   This is a skull from a pug, although you may guess it is from another brachycephalic breed.

4.   This skull looks very squashed up with a classic appearance of that belonging to a brachycephalic breed. The eye sockets are also wide and large which correlates to the 'pop eyed' appearance of pugs. Also note how the nose is completely squashed up along the top of the maxilla.

5.   The design of the pug unfortunately predisposes it to many health conditions; you may mention that because all of the skull features are there but squashed up this often makes the breed likely to suffer from BOAS (brachycephalic obstructive airway syndrome). The eye sockets are wide but shallow which also means the eyeball does not sit well within the orbit, therefore often pugs can suffer from traumatic problems relating to their eyes due to the way they are sat in the skull. You may even mention the teeth and how all the teeth are squashed up too, and mention how this can relate to dental problems which pugs are prone to.

Good answer In a good answer, the candidate would:

- **Correctly identify structure and state what breed it is from**
- **Realise the potential health problems,** just from looking at the structure and using initiative to explain how the way the skull is adapted can cause problems.
- **Continually explain their thought process,** to help them reach their decisions.

Poor answer In a poor answer, the candidate might:

- **Offer superficial detail and fail to go into depth** - E.g. They only say they see a skull but cannot explain why they think that.
- **Fail to attempt a guess at potential health problems even if prompted with phrases** - E.g. They may ask if this looks like a normal dog skull.
- **Be unable to offer justification for why they think the structure is a particular part** - In this case, a good candidate should relate the anatomy to BOAS. For example, just saying that a skull has dental crowding is not enough - they need to say why this anatomical change has occurred.

Expert's Advice

Every time you say a statement or make a point ask yourself "why?" This will help you develop your answer and it is what the interviewer is looking for.

CHAPTER 7

VII Veterinary ethics

7.1 Introduction

Ethics surrounding veterinary medicine is a topical area which you will come across all throughout your studies and during practice. A lot of it is about finding out what your own views are as there is no 'correct' answer. Therefore, questions surrounding veterinary ethics are almost always part of the interview process.

Researching ethics

In order to fully understand the ethics question being asked and give a good answer, candidates need to ensure they are well researched on the topic which is being asked. Here is a list of hot topics which you may face in your interview.

- Foxhunting ban
- Badger culling
- Carrying 'toy' breeds in handbags/ dressing them up
- Breeding dogs for flat faces (brachycephalic breeds)
- Deciding not to spay/ neuter your pet
- Deciding not to vaccinate your pet
- Feeding a raw diet
- Euthanizing animals
- Uses of animal in labs
- Animals in the food chain
- Veganism
- Animals in science - testing them for human drugs
- Poaching of wild animals
- Captive bred animals in zoos
- Dog/ cat breeders
- Doping of horses for races
- Use of hormonal injections/ implants in dairy cows
- Farrowing crates
- Slaughtering of animals
- Keeping wild animals as pets
- Veal production
- Foie gras production
- Salmon farming
- microplastics / plastic pollution in the ocean
- Fur farms
- Climate change
- Religion and ethics

Expert's Advice

Make sure when researching on these topics you use trusted resources which provide fact and not opinion based literature. The BBC website, scientific journals (from ScienceDirect and Pubmed) are more reliable and will give you a better understanding than media based charities such as PETA or the RSPCA.

When researching ethical issues, it is important to try and have an argument for both sides. For example, if we take caring toy breeds in handbags from above, it is wise to have some points to say why some people may think this is bad for welfare as it compromises the 5 freedoms (we will come back to this under animal welfare), and then have a counter argument of 'but the dog is very well looked after and so not all 5 freedoms are compromised and the owner may not understand this'. This shows your interviewer that you have thoroughly researched the topic, and can deliver information in an unbiased manner - something which is very important to being a vet.

Justifying your ethical reasoning

During this part of the interview, the interviewer is not looking for the 'correct' answer or whether you agree with them. Rather, they are looking to see how good you are at rationalising and giving a balanced argument. You will be marked down if you have a one sided view on the matter or if you sound like you are trying to persuade the interviewer. It is much better to have a balanced view and to not come across as pushy or judgemental to those who disagree with your view.

To help give reasoning you need to display your empathy (remember that buzzword!?) and think not just how you would feel if you swapped places with that person, but how those factors relating to that person makes them feel in the situation. This shows a high degree of emotional intelligence which is important for vets and also shows the interviewer maturity and rationality with regards to your answer.

Some factors of those involved which may help rationalise your view may be:

Someone's age
Are younger people more easily influenced by the media? Or have they grown up to have the same ethical views and practices as their parents/ carers?

Religion
Bear in mind that different religions have different views on animal ethics, particularly surrounding slaughtering procedures/ halal meat / species they do/ do not eat. This is a very important topic to research.

Culture
Different countries have different beliefs on animal ethics and slaughtering procedures.

Dietary requirements
Are the ethical issues you are debating related to vegetarianism/ veganism, why might someone have chosen those dietary choices?

Views on animals
Another difficult pill to swallow as someone who loves animals, is the realisation that not everybody loves animals. There are people out there who see animals as pests, nuisances, and vermin. These people undoubtedly will hold different views when compared with someone who wants to be a vet.

Past experiences
Does a person hold a particular view because they have had a previous experience relating to the ethical issues/ animals in question? This may be something to consider too.

Sample responses

Is badger culling the answer to fighting bovine TB?

"No, as no animal should be wrongfully killed for no good reason as in my opinion that is very unethical. Instead we should ask farmers to report badger sightings so we can apply the badger vaccination programme. This means that the badgers and cows both live without being harmed."

Feedback

This is a poor answer. It does not show a great deal of empathy when considering the farm. Their view on animals will be much different as they need to protect their cattle for their livelihood. This answer also is very one sided and does not give a balanced view on why the culling is potentially beneficial to the farmers, it just considers the badgers and so is a quite immature answer.

"Although animal euthanasia should be seen as a last resort, controlling bacterial infection in cattle is a priority to prevent zoonotic transmission to farmers, improving cattle welfare, and reducing the cost of the livestock industry. Farmers will most likely agree that badger culling is the answer to fighting TB in their cattle. This is because their cattle is their income and to them badgers are seen as pests on their land who need to be culled in order to save their cows and their livelihoods. Therefore, considering the farmers' views but also respecting the fact that badgers are a protected species I think that more care should go into reservoir control. One study found that transmission of mycobacterium bovis is more likely to occur within species rather than between species. Therefore, as TB will spread through badgers easier we need to stop the transmission at this point so it doesn't become an issue for cattle. This could possibly be via targeted badger vaccination programmes in the areas of England most affected - for example in the southwest of England. Thus meaning that accurate badger vaccination as a form of reservoir control may be the answer to fighting bovine TB'.

Feedback

This is an excellent answer. The student considers how the farmer will be feeling on this issue and how his views will be different from other people surrounding this topic. The student then goes on to give their own opinion with accurate scientific evidence to back this up by a study. Although there are some drawbacks of vaccinating which the student does not mention, they go on to justify how to get the best out of doing this programme to combat TB.

Practice MMI station

Station brief

You are a new graduate vet in a small, privately owned practice who is on call out of hours. You receive a call from an owner that is not registered with the practice to say their pet has been hit by a car. However, they explain to you that they have severe cost restrictions and are likely to struggle to pay for any treatment.

Discuss the different factors involved in this scenario and what you might do.

Good   answer   A   good   answer   may   include:

• Thinking about the different **stakeholders** involved. Whilst your first instinct may be to think of an animal who is likely suffering (and this is certainly important), what about how the owner is feeling about this situation? What about the owner of your practice, who relies on its income for their livelihood? And crucially what about you? How do you think you would feel in this situation if it happened in real life?

• Knowing your **legal responsibilities**. The RCVS code of conduct says that we have a legal obligation to provide first aid in cases like this, but this can mean different things to different people. At the very least we should be offering pain relief to make this animal comfortable, or if we do not feel this is possible then suggesting euthanasia if there is no other option.

• **Communication** is vital in situations such as this. Remaining calm and explaining clearly to the owners what you can and can't do in advance ensures realistic expectations. This is a highly stressful situation for both you and the owners and things could easily become heated if communication breaks down.

Poor answer A poor answer may include:

• Being **judgemental**. As a vet you are likely to interact with all sorts of people from all sorts of backgrounds. It can be easy to think 'these people shouldn't have got a dog if they couldn't afford to care for it'. This may be true, but it is not our job to make such judgements, we must do what is best for the animal whenever this occurs.

• **Rushing** into things. Emergency situations can be very nerve-wracking, and it can be easy to make decisions quickly. We need to carry out a detailed assessment of the animal in front of us to work out what, if anything, can be done. Otherwise, we may actually end up costing our practice more money than we need to.

• Creating **unrealistic expectations.** Given the lack of finances in this case, there will be lots of scenarios where we are unable to cure the animal involved. However, as long as we can keep the animal comfortable overnight, it may be that the owners can source funds from elsewhere or we can refer them to a charity practice for further treatment.

7.2 Animal welfare

Introduction

Tied closely with veterinary ethics, animal welfare is something that your answer to interview questions should always consider given as when you are a vet you will be making decisions to not compromise an animal's welfare. Animal welfare is a very broad topic and comprises lots of peoples varying opinions so in order to give a good answer in your interview, you need to ensure you are equipped to give a balanced and non judgemental answer - similar to veterinary ethics.

The 5 freedoms

As mentioned before, the five freedoms act almost as the basis when assessing animal welfare. Introduced in 1941, they can be applied to any animal in any given situation to assess their welfare. They are as follows.

1. Freedom from hunger, thirst and malnutrition
2. Freedom from thermal and physical discomfort
3. Freedom from pain, injury and disease
4. Freedom from fear and distress
5. Freedom to express normal behaviour

When given an animal welfare/ethical MMI station or question, running through each of the 5 freedoms is a good way to give a balanced answer. It also shows you have done research into animal welfare - a major component of the veterinary medicine course.

Timing Tip

Don't feel the need to mention and assess every single one of the 5 freedoms. By mentioning 1 or 2 (usually as a balancing the argument point) you will have covered enough basis to let the interviewer know you are clued up on the 5 freedoms and have a good understanding of animal welfare.

Duty of care concept

Another aspect to consider when assessing and talking about animal welfare in your interview is the duty of care concept. The duty of care concept in an animal welfare sense means if you are responsible for an animal, you have a duty of care for the animal regardless of why you are responsible for that animal, the animal's purpose or how long you will care for that animal.

Relating a situation to the duty of care concept is a good way to consider how different people from different cultures, backgrounds and with different ages etc will view animal welfare.

Sample responses

Here is an image taken in Brazil where the slaughter and consumption of most dogs is legal.

Discuss issues surrounding this image

"This image is greatly upsetting to me as someone who wants to go into a career caring for animals by improving their welfare. I think it is disgusting how dogs are used for the meat trade in some countries as we have bred dogs to be pets, not to be eaten for human consumption. I think that making the slaughter and consumption of dog illegal in Brazil and counties where this occurs is the biggest issue which needs to be tackled in order to improve the welfare of these animals"

Feedback

This is a poor answer. Although this student mentions how animal welfare is not really considered here, they only mention this in relation to their own opinion of disagreeing with dog meat consumption. They don't consider the implications of the conditions that the animals are in on their current welfare; in fact they don't relate back to the image once apart from letting the interviewer know it has upset them. Additionally, they come across as ignorant of other people's cultures.

Common Pitfall

It is important to refer back to the image when given a picture station/question. Use the fact you have a visual aid to guide you in order to get the most out of answering the question. Referring directly to the image by picking aspects out from it lets the interviewer know you understood the question and are observant.

In this image, one issue I can clearly see is that the welfare of these animals is compromised. Thinking about the 5 freedoms, it is more than likely that the dogs in this image are not free from pain, injury and disease. I can tell this because the metal cage they are housed in looks dirty and is rusting which could make the dogs at risk of infection. This risk is definitely heightened by the fact there are multiple dogs in one cage meaning the risk of disease transmission increases. Adding on to this the dogs fur doesn't look too clean which also comprises their freedom of physical discomfort. Although there are clearly animal welfare issues at hand, this should have nothing to do with the trade these dogs are in. Considering the duty of care concept, those responsible for the care of these dogs should give them accurate care and ensure they have their 5 freedoms. Just because they are being slaughtered for meat does not mean their welfare should be disregarded".

Feedback

This is an excellent answer. This response actually refers back to the image in order to relate it to the 5 freedoms in order to assess the welfare of these animals. The answer also considers the duty of care concept which shows to the interviewer that the candidate is respectful of the culture behind an animal's use in certain cultures and societies in the world.

Practice MMI station

Station brief

The 5 Freedoms have been a long established guide in Veterinary practice and welfare. They are listed below:

1. Freedom from hunger and thirst
2. Freedom from discomfort
3. Freedom from pain, injury and disease
4. Freedom to express normal behaviour
5. Freedom from fear and distress

Imagine you work at a rescue shelter. Someone would like to adopt a rabbit. Explain to them factors they should consider if they would like to bring home a rabbit with specific examples using the given 5 freedoms.

Good answer A good answer may include:

- Sound understand and interpretation of the 5 freedoms
- Translation of the freedoms into every day practice for a pet rabbit e.g.
  - Rabbit should always have access to food and water
  - Rabbit should be housed in an appropriate shelter and bedding
  - Rabbit should be cared for intently and should be taken to the vet if any health issues arise
  - Rabbit should be able to express behaviours such as gnawing, running and playing. Best answer will mention the use of ENRICHMENT to provide stimulation, and housing in pairs.
  - Rabbit should not be threatened by predators or stressful situations.
- Be friendly and concise while using accessible language.
- Notice that the scenario is set in a rescue shelter, so students must use words such as "adopt" or "rescue" rather than "buy". Students may mention implications of adopting a rabbit over buying one from a breeder e.g. rabbit may be more nervous or older but they still require the same care.

Poor answer A poor answer may include:

- Lack of understanding of the 5 freedoms e.g. simply repeating them rather than attempting to interpret them.
- Lack of communication skills e.g. using inappropriate language for the setting. Students must remember they are speaking to a member of the public who may not have any prior knowledge of rabbit housing or welfare implications.
- All 5 freedoms not covered or attempted.
- Do not try to convince the person who wants to adopt a rabbit that they should or should not do so. Students' answers must be balanced, factual and unbiased.

7.3 Euthanasia

Introduction

Given that euthanasia is extremely relevant to veterinary practice, is a hot ethical topic and something you probably will have seen in your small animal work experience this is a topic which you are likely to talk about in your interview.

What actually happens when euthanizing an animal

Although there are many definitions of animal euthanasia, it can be described as 'the act of putting a painless, quick death to an animal.' Usually, most clients will bring their pets in with the mindset that the vet is about to euthanize them. Before anything medical can be administered, vets need to obtain consent from their owner which is usually done via a forum with the vet explaining the next steps from the drugs to cremation etc.

When the euthanasia is about to begin, the vet should talk the client through every stage. First, the fur of the animal is clipped away, this is followed by an intravenous injection which at first may startle the animal. Then the vet will administer anaesthetic drugs which overdose the animal until they become unconscious and eventually their heart stops.

How the client will act and what the vet should do

Understanding this will be a distressing time for the owners of the pet. In certain cases, some clients may not understand why euthanasia is necessary and therefore the vet will have to explain. Most if not all clients will not have a good understanding of medical terms so make sure to convey this in a way they will.

Euthanizing an animal costs the practice money and therefore this needs to be discussed with the client. Some clients may want to pay before the event so they can leave as soon as it is over, others may wish to pay in the consultant room rather than going back out into reception. Therefore, it is important that the vet discusses this with the client before any medical intervention of the patient.

It is also a good idea to send a condolence card to the client which can help grieving owners or can give owners who feel guilty for pursuing euthanasia a deal of comfort.

The key during this event is to always be empathetic without being overly emotional. Clients want to feel confident in the fact that you are euthanizing their pet. You can portray this by speaking to the animal by name and letting owners have time with the body without your presence. Many owners will feel comforted in the fact that you can offer them the animal collar or a lock of its hair.

Issues surrounding euthanasia

Euthanasia is a very sensitive topic and many multiplying factors are involved in why an animal is going to be euthanized. The decision from the vet to euthanize a patient manifests in different decision outcomes.

Absolutely justified euthanasia - This includes severe skeletal trauma in working animals (long bone fractures) and catastrophic head/spinal injury in companion animals.

Even though euthanasia in this case is necessary, the vet still must receive consent from the owner. If consent is not given (which can happen), the vet must consider what action to take as the next step. This may be perhaps getting a second opinion from another vet in the practice of communicating in a different manner why euthanasia is necessary. If consent is still refused the RCVS (Royal college of veterinary surgeons) can be contacted for further advice.

Contextually justified euthanasia - This may be when an animal has unpredictable aggression towards children or persistent and chronic anxiety and social isolation.

For this type of euthanasia, the vet and client need to fully consider the welfare of the animal as well as the client and other members of the public. Alos for this type of euthanasia communication is key as for example an animal may be needed euthanasia in this case because the owner is not providing basic care, so instead of euthanasia it is possible to educate the owner instead or in worse cases resort them to the police.

Non-justified euthanasia- This may include a situation where an owner will not consider rehoming a healthy animal.

In this instance, the vet feels the act of euthanasia is not justified in the case of the animals welfare. Killing the animal is unnecessary so the vet will offer second hand opinions and other advice on how the client can deal with the animal they brought in. For example, a vet may recommend rehousing the animal to a friend of the client, if the client still refuses this and wants to have their animal euthanized then legally as their vet you can refuse to euthanize if you feel it is non-justified. Once again in this case, the RCVS can be consulted for advice.

Decision tree

As there are a lot of issues surrounding euthanasia of animals, below is a figure form the BVA (British Veterinary Association). It allows you to go through different rational reasonings which may result in your decision to euthanize.

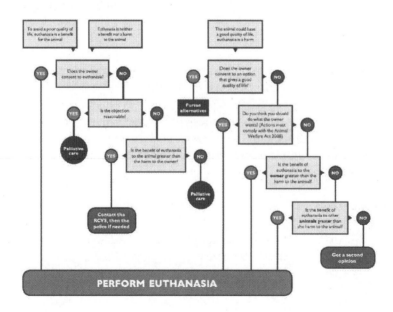

Consider the following cases and assess whether you would euthanize the animal at hand.

- Owned but unwanted healthy animals.
- Owned terminally ill, suffering animal; owner wants euthanasia.
- Owned terminally ill, suffering animal; owner refuses euthanasia.
- Owned terminally ill, mildly suffering animal; owner refuses euthanasia; owner very attached.
- Owned terminally ill, suffering animal; owner not available.
- Owned animal with illness with minor effect on quality of life—for example, mild heart failure; owner wants euthanasia.
- Owned healthy animal with incontinence/ minor behavioural problem—owner requests euthanasia.
- Unowned wild animal with major injuries.
- Unowned wild non-indigenous species (for example, grey squirrel).
- Injured wild non-indigenous/pest species.

Expert's Advice

The main aspect which the interviewer is looking to see in your answer is can you rationalise. They want to know you have the animals best interest and are considering their animal welfare whilst also respecting the client's wishes and feelings.

7.4 Practice Questions: Ethics

1. Do you believe that euthanasia should be allowed?
2. What are the benefits of euthanasia?
3. What are the issues with euthanasia?
4. Should people be allowed to keep pets if they can't afford veterinary care?
5. Why can't vets give a guarantee that a medical or surgical procedure will be successful?
6. Why should breeders be allowed to breed animals when there are lots of pets in rescue centres?
7. Should horses be allowed to race?
8. Should a mentally ill client be allowed to keep their pets, if they are unable to look after them?
9. Is it right not to vaccinate your pet, if you do nott believe that vaccinations work?
10. What should you do if a client refuses to pay for their pet's treatment?
11. Why can selective breeding be good and bad?
12. What are the problems with designer dog breeds?
13. What are the major issues with brachycephalic dog breeds?
14. What are the differences between length of life and quality of life?
15. How does the media influence trends in dog breeds?
16. Should veterinary care be free?
17. How are farm animals treated differently to pet animals?
18. What are the different purposes of farm and pet animals?
19. Is it right to cull farm animals that have a slower productivity? (E.g. laying hens that don't lay eggs anymore)
20. Is it fair to slaughter animals for human consumption?

CHAPTER 8

VIII Human-Animal bond

8.1 Introduction

To help answer the above questions and almost any question relating to an animal and their owner, the human-animal bond will be discussed in this section.

The human-animal bond is a mutually beneficial and dynamic relationship between people and animals which is influenced by behaviours essential to the health and well-being of both. It is no surprise that dogs and cats specifically are an integral part of modern society providing companionship, security and nutrition experiences for many so it's even less surprising that clients put their trust in vets to respect the bond they share with their pet and for you to make them better.

The human-animal bond is the backbone of the veterinary care which you will be giving to your patients, essentially without this bond you would have less clientele at small animal practice. The human-animal bond is also an interesting aspect of assessing how humans view animals which is a key concept assessed in vet school interviews as the interviewer wants to see how you view animals which will be in your care; whether this be a beloved family pet, prized racehorse or beef production cattle.

8.2 Human-animal bond: Pets

As just discussed, companion animals can provide a lot to a person. Pet ownership has been associated with higher levels of physical activity, lower blood pressure and reduced incidence of stress and depression in humans. You may have witnessed in your clinical work experience that owners are willing to spend a lot of money and ensure they have the best veterinary health care for their pets. This is due to their strong-human animal bond; they see their animal as one of the family.

Similar to pets are some small working animals such as labradors for the blind or dogs and cats as emotional support animals. As with bets, this same strong human-animal bond is shared as these animals are able to provide security and assistance to those who are vulnerable.

8.3 Human-animal bond: Working animals

Racehorses are sometimes commonly and notoriously euthanised if they can no longer race. It is important to note that if a companion dog was no longer able to walk most owners will go to great lengths for medication and rehabilitation to ensure their pets animal welfare is optimised. However most of the time with racing horses there is less of a human-animal bond as their owner mainly views them to win the race to make money - not as a companion. Therefore, euthanasia is considered here more often than submitting the horse to a rehabilitation centre as there is a smaller degree of the human-animal bond.

More commonly in non-western countries, animals such as donkeys, alpacas and even elephants are used to transport and carry goods long distances. In this instance the human-animal bond here is purely based on the service which that animal can supply the owner of that animal. This does not necessarily mean there is poor animal welfare, it is just a different type of human-animal bond than seen in companion animals.

8.4 Human-animal bond: Production animals

In the UK and the rest of the world, a lot of larger farm animals such as cows, sheep, pigs as well as poultry are solely used for the production of meat, dairy and eggs. Many workers in the meat production sector such as farmers or abattoir staff don't have a strong connection to this animal as they are seen purely as a product. Even members of the public may share these thoughts: the fact that cows are for consumption but dogs are for companions.

As the human-animal bond is less strong, a lot of aspects of maintaining and rearing animals for meat are seen by many as not in their best interest of welfare.

For example, in the UK most sows (female pigs) are housed in farrowing crates for around 5 weeks. Farrowing crates allow the sow to drink and feed but not move and she just stays on her side allowing her piglets to suckele.The point of farrowing crates is to protect the piglets from being crushed by the sow. When the piglets are first born, they are very small and fragile and in free sow stalls (where the sow's movement is not restricted) the piglet mortality greatly increases.

Although this is initially seen as not in the best animal welfare for the sow, the farmer has to think of all the piglets (usually 9) involved and the fact that he has to keep them alive so he can grow and sell them. Therefore, farrowing crates use a utilitarianism viewpoint (greatest amount of good animal welfare for the greatest number of animals)whereby the sow is suffering but the piglets benefit (the suffering of the minority for the benefit of the majority = utilitarianism).

Although the animals' end purpose is slaughter, up until this point their welfare should not be compromised and should always be checked and assessed to be in the best case scenario for that animal. Use this next MMI station to see how to approach a question thinking about this.

Practice MMI station

Station brief

You are a vet student on placement at a local dairy farm.

Every evening when taking the cows in for milking the farmers' son shouts abuse at the cows for not moving fast enough. He hits many of the cows across the back end with a pipe, marking some of them in the process. He tends to ignore you when you offer to help. You are unsure what to do.

What should you do next?

Good   answer   A   good   answer   may   include:

- **Recognise the complexity of the situation.** It is important for any response to be reasoned and calculated. Taking a step back to recognise all stakeholders involved in the situation before responding is crucial. In this case, the stakeholders are the farmer, the farmer's son, and you, the student. A good candidate may recognise that the farmer's son has acted this way by explaining the human-animal bond between production animals.
- **Animal Welfare.** Acknowledge that animal welfare is unnecessarily compromised here. The actions of the farmer's son are inappropriate. You may mention the 5 needs of animal welfare, most prominently the need to be free from pain. Students will take note that just because the human-animal bond of these animals is not the same as a companion animal, this does not mean they should be treated differently.
- **Action.** An overall assessment of the situation is needed here. As a student, it is not your place to teach the farmer's son that his actions are unacceptable. Best practice is to report the details of the incident back to your University placement manager, and allow them to take any further action, as deemed necessary. If you feel unsafe on the placement, they will allow you to leave.

Poor answer In a poor answer, a candidate may suggest:

- **Intervening immediately without consideration.** This station tests the ability of the candidate to use sound reasoning when presented with an emotionally difficult situation. To confront the farmer's son about the situation would be likely unproductive, as he clearly has little interest in interacting with the student. Answers including reporting the farmer's son to the RSPCA would also be too drastic.
- **Doing nothing.** It is important for the student to recognise that what is happening is wrong, and that animal welfare is being compromised.
- **Inappropriate action.** Reporting the situation and/or posting pictures/videos of it on social media would be entirely inappropriate and would go against social media policy for Vet students.

CHAPTER 9

IX Logistics

9.1 What to wear for the interview

Introduction

Surprisingly, this is a step which candidates who have received an interview stress the most about - it's not something you can study after all. It is more than likely that, at this point in your life, this interview is the most important formal interview you have ever had, and of course you want to make a good impression as soon as you walk through the door.

Interviewer's perspective

As discussed at the start of this booklet, vet school interviews can often feel very conversational. The interviewer will do their best to make you feel as relaxed as possible, as they want to get to know you to see if you are the right fit for their vet school. Whilst keeping to a smart casual dress code, your choice of clothing is a great way to show the interviewers a bit of your personality.

What shall I wear?

As the dress code is smart casual, it is most typical and easiest for men to wear suits. This will typically be navy or black and will be a suit of its simplest form - no waistcoat or small accessories. After all, it is important you also feel comfortable and are not worrying about what you are wearing.

For girls there is definitely more flexibility. Girls can absolutely go for the suit option as well or others tend to go even more casual with a blouse and smart trousers; a skirt is equally fine as long as it is worn with tights.

It also is a good idea to think about practicality. Some vet schools will give a tour of their campus before sitting down to interview. As this will likely be during winter/autumn months, make sure you wrap up if appropriate and wear comfortable and suitable shoes.

The Do's and Don'ts
Do

- Dress smart or smart casually, depending on the university requests
- Bring a jacket, preferably rain proof, and something to keep warm
- Do show your personal style, while remaining smart casual

Don't

- Wear high heels and other uncomfortable shoes for walking
- Avoid dresses or skirts that are likely to blow up in the wind
- Spend a fortune on a designer outfit

Common Pitfall

Definitely do nott stress too much about your outfit and ensure it is comfortable. When you are being put on the spot for an interview, what you are wearing is going to be the last thing you want to be thinking about. So just remember: smart, casual and comfortable.

9.2 Planning your route

Introduction

If your interview is in person, then you have the opportunity to visit the city and more importantly the vet school. For many candidates, this may mean you need to travel - sometimes quite far.

Travelling

Make sure you leave enough time for the possibility that something may go wrong in your journey. If you are travelling by train, make sure you know in advance if there are any train strikes / works on the railway line you are taking. It is best to get the train to your destination a day or even two before your interview. This way, if there are any delays or cancellations you will not miss your interview.

Additionally, getting to the city a day or two before is beneficial as you have time to explore and take in a potential home for the next 5 years!

Likewise, if travelling via car, ensure all motorway routes are open and leave enough time in case something goes wrong. The last thing you want to do after so much preparation is be late!

Expert's Advice

Most vet schools interview over a number of days with some vet schools even giving you a selected number of days you can choose from. Make sure you do your travelling research before you pick your interview day. If you are given a date you physically are unable to travel on, don't be afraid to email the vet school to let them know.

9.3 Final and last minute tips for the day

Introduction

Although this book is designed to relieve any anxiety for your interview, it is only normal to get nervous on the run up to your interview day.

Here are a few last minute tips to think about in the final hours before your interview.

A good night's sleep

You want to feel fresh and ready to take on the interview the next morning. Make sure the night before you get your head down and get a good and well deserved rest for the big day.

Do not overdo last minute prep

Similar to getting sleep, do not keep yourself awake all night going over your notes and reading the student room for what the interview might be like. If you do this, your brain is not going to get a rest and it is possible you will forget everything you tried to cram the night before! Reading some conclusive notes before sleep is a good idea but not every aspect of veterinary medicine.

Know the itinerary

You may be feeling anxious about what you are going to be doing in the day and where you are going or need to be. By printing out the itinerary (or if it has not been sent, asking the vet school for one) you can be prepared for what you will be doing on the day.

Staying relaxed

Easier said than done! The best thing you can do right before and in the lead up to your interview is to remind yourself that you have got this! Make a relaxing playlist to listen to on the journey to the vet school, or write yourself a note reminding yourself you are going to ace the interview. You could even speak to a family member or friend to get some reassurance - whatever you need to get yourself into a positive and calm mindset!

9.4 Conclusion

Overview

This book has covered almost everything which may appear in your interview for veterinary medicine, along with tips and advice on how to score highly against other candidates. By going through the interview structure, what questions may be used, and samples of how to best answer these questions, this booklet is one of the best ways to be prepared for your interview!

Final tips

- Make sure to use all of the sample questions and MMI stations to practise your interview technique. You can even give the questions to a parent or teacher to run a face-to-face mock interview!
- Go over the expert advice, common pitfalls and timing tips before and after answering a practice question. With each practice question, use the tips in this book to evaluate what went well and how you could improve your answer next time.
- Don't just go over what you find easiest! Remember you will be asked an array of questions, all of which this book covers. If you find answering a question about ethics harder than a question about personal qualities, you should allocate more time to practising the former as this is where you need the most work. You may not have a lot of time between receiving your interview invitation and your actual interview date, so be wise about timing your revision. Creating a timetable that outlines how much time you will spend preparing for each topic, and when, will help your preparation go a lot smoother.

Good luck!

Good luck with your interview for veterinary medicine! We hope this booklet has helped you feel more relaxed and prepared about going into your interview. Here at medic mind we want students to not only excel in their interview but also to enjoy it!

You can find more free resources on the Medic Mind Blog - https://www.medicmind.co.uk/medicine-ucas-guide/topic/veterinary-medicine-interviews/

We also offer a comprehensive online course for the veterinary medicine interview, if you prefer to work independently (https://www.medicmind.co.uk/veterinary-medicine-interview-course/) and 1:1 tutoring for the interview if you want some additional, tailored support (https://www.medicmind.co.uk/vet-interview-tutors/)

With numerous insider tips and tricks along with practice questions and MMI stations the 'Vet interview booklet' is brought to you by Medic Mind, an award winning company of vets and vet students who tutor students through vet school applications here in the UK and beyond! Having helped over 10,000 students with their GCSEs, A-levels, UCAT, BMAT, interview, personal statement and more we are proud to bring this experience to more students. An updated 2022 version of your guide to your veterinary medicine interview.

1:1 VET INTERVIEW TUTORING

 Delivered by current Vet students, who have excelled in the interview themselves

 A personalised 1:1 approach, tailored to your unique needs

 Learn how to answer questions on motivation, skills, work experience, veterinary ethics, anatomy, and more

EXCLUSIVE OFFER: GET 70% OFF YOUR FIRST LESSON

Book a free consultation today to unlock this offer by visiting www.medicmind.co.uk/vet-interview-tutors/ or scan the QR code below

VET INTERVIEW ONLINE COURSE

 Video tutorials, designed by our Vet interview experts, to guide you through the most common question topics

 Top tips and techniques to construct the perfect interview answers under time pressure

 Model answers and practice questions to aid you in your preparation

EXCLUSIVE OFFER: GET 10% OFF USING THE CODE BOOK10

Find out more at www.medicmind.co.uk/veterinary-medicine-interview-online-course-2023/ or scan the QR code below

Made in the USA
Las Vegas, NV
18 November 2024

12084802R00057